TRUE CONFESSIONS
OF A REAL MR. MOM

True Confessions of a Real Mr. Mom

By

Mark Wertman

Writer's Showcase
San Jose New York Lincoln Shanghai

True Confessions of a Real Mr. Mom

Published by Writer's Showcase,
an imprint of iUniverse.com, Inc.

For information address:
iUniverse.com, Inc.
620 North 48th Street
Suite 201
Lincoln, NE 68504-3467
www.iuniverse.com

ISBN: 0-595-00046-0

A Son to His Mother and Father

In the middle of the night I still wake up, sometimes from a dream that has left me frightened. I sit up in bed, and I remember how the two of you would comfort me, hold me and tell me everything would be okay, and it was. As you both continue to be there for me in my adult life, your goodness shines throughout, and your hearts remain the purest of hearts I have ever known.

A Husband to His Wife

From the moment you are born there is another person out there who will allow you to see the great light within yourself, and all around you. When the two of you join as one, that new reality comes true. That person, whomever it might be, is truly considered your other half. I found my new reality when I met you, my dear wife. Here's to you, my puzzle piece, my light to perceive the wonders of this glorious world.

A Father to His Children

Since all of you came into my life, you have awakened my senses. My taste is sweeter. My sight is clearer. Life seems more fragrant. I hear harmonies that I had never imagined existed. You have each touched my heart, and now my heart touches all. But there's something more—an awakened combined sense. It is the sense of belonging, the sense of true family, the sense of a love that will last beyond my last breath. Thank you all,

Love, your Daddy.

Contents

Acknowledgements

For critical reading of the manuscript and other forms of advice and counsel, I am very grateful to Sarah Sabag, Carolyn Lieberman, Sara Ullman, Victoria Wilheim, Sheryl Horowitz and Debbie Pottins. Special thanks to my supportive, encouraging family members and friends.

In the Beginning

Once upon a time there were two people. Their names were Adam and Eve. They lived in a beautiful garden. This garden had everything that the two people needed, but after a while they grew tired of paradise.

One day, Eve set out to find the meaning of life and met a very knowledgeable, quite eclectic snake. As I intimated in my last statement, the snake was very smart and passed on his knowledge about certain things to Eve; I think it was through some sort of fruit—maybe an apple. Eve perked up right away and realized that she was missing out on many things. There was a whole world out there with fancy cars, big houses and lots of jewelry that she had to have. So she went to Adam and told him to eat some of the apple and procure a good-paying job.

Adam responded immediately to what Eve had said, and a couple of weeks later Adam secured himself a mid-level management position in the garden. Shortly after that, Adam and Eve decided to have a child. They named the child Cain. Adam was relatively well paid, but he did not earn enough to afford the extras. So, Eve decided that since she was as smart as Adam, (after all, she did eat from the same apple) she was going to get a job too, so they could have it all. But what about Cain?

Eve went to seek out the snake's wisdom on this question, and to her surprise, the snake was a childcare professional. He told her not to worry; he would be delighted to take care of Cain. Eve was very happy.

Since Eve had known the snake on some level, she didn't bother to check his references.

Eve had another child named Abel a few years later and things were not working out with the care the snake was giving to Cain. Cain was repeating things only the snake could have taught him and this was distressing Adam and Eve. Eve started hearing, through the grapevine, many disconcerting things about the snake. So Eve decided to give up her job and stay home with her sons, in order to be very attentive to them. Unfortunately, she was too late to help Cain. When the two boys grew up, things didn't work out very well. I think we all know how the story turned out.

1

MY BEGINNING

HUSH-A-BYE

HUSH-A-BYE, BABY,
LIE STILL WITH YOUR DADDY,
YOUR MOMMY HAS GONE TO THE MILL.
TO GET SOME MEAL TO BAKE A CAKE,
SO PLEASE, MY DEAR BABY, LIE STILL.

January, 1996
New Jersey
Carpool

The alarm rings, piercing the quiet of the dark room. *Oh no, I* groaned, *it's not possible. It can't be seven already. I've got to get myself together. I have to get the kids up and make their lunches. Shit! I've got to drive carpool today. Georgina left for work already? That means waking Becky up. She's going to be miserable all day and since misery loves company, this day is not going to be one of my best. Someone, throw me a life preserver, or please, let the sharks eat me quickly. Come on Mark, get yourself up! The kids are going to be late.*

Every morning it was the same thing. Get the kids up, get them off to school, shopping, cooking, cleaning, laundry, and running the many errands that one person couldn't possibly get done in the few hours left before the children came home. There were so many responsibilities, obligations and commitments in running my home. I was SOOOO tired. I was in such a rut. There had to be more to life. I had to under-stand why? Why did I become a Mr. Mom?

January 24th, 1988
Los Angeles, California
The Birth Of A New Road

The day Gabriella was born I already knew that I would be a stay-at-home dad; it was decided by economics. My wife Georgina was an attorney and made a good living; I was a struggling songwriter. We had agreed early in our marriage that nobody other than one of us would stay at home and raise our children. What I didn't know was what was in store for me in my newfound career. I had no idea how much work it would be to take care of one child, and subsequently, how that was a mere pittance compared to the three children I now have. But let me go back to when life was simpler, when it was just Georgina, Gabriella and myself.

After Georgina went back to work, the first few days of staying home alone with Gabriella were a big adjustment. Not only did I have to take care of the baby, but also Georgina. It was a significant emotional adjustment for her to return to work, which required enormous amounts of attention from me. Georgina working made logical sense, but it was very hard on her and I felt terribly guilty. I was the "man", gonads and all, and I had been taught that I should be the one who worked, made the money, brought home the bacon, or if you're a vegetarian, maybe the broccoli. I guess it was leftover teachings from the cave. My genetically-programmed role was to drag my mate home by the hair, go out and kill that night's dinner and then come home and see what new drawings of current sporting events there were on the cave wall.

The first real task that I had was to make sure Georgina was closely involved in all aspects of child rearing. I didn't want her to feel left out or to create a situation where she believed that her only job was to go to work and the children were solely my responsibility. That result would have not been good for any of us.

I decided at first to go to her office every day and meet her for lunch. This not only gave her a chance to see Gabriella, but it was also a necessity. At first, Gabriella was not that cooperative in taking a bottle. She only wanted the breast, and I was in way over my head in that department. Being completely under-equipped with the right amount of hormones in that area, I would drive to Georgina's work every day, racing up to her office for the afternoon feeding.

I remember standing in front of Georgina's office door while she was feeding Gabriella. I was like a bouncer at a hot nightclub and since there was a private party going on, I set a policy of "no entry allowed," but they still tried. I was a firsthand witness to how persistent lawyers could be in gaining access to very personal information about anything and everything. After a couple of days they finally got the message—when I was there, they should LEAVE GEORGINA ALONE!

Another beneficial thing about meeting Georgina for lunch was that we could talk about how she was feeling with regard to work. My intent was to integrate her work life into our home life. I thought it was very important that we were in a partnership all the way, whether it was regarding the kids or our chosen professions.

I think it's all a part of communicating with each other. To give you some background, when Georgina and I were married she made it very clear that she preferred that we not have a TV in the bedroom. I asked her why. This was contrary to what my parents did and, quite frankly, I thought it was an American tradition. I didn't see anything wrong with tirelessly surfing the many channels that television has to offer so I could be peacefully lulled to sleep when I couldn't find anything I truly wanted to watch.

She was very insistent. She said this simple sacrifice would insure that we always communicated: we would talk about our lives, current events, friends, family, whatever came up, instead of passively watching others do things, either real or fictional, on television.

I have to admit that to this day (and it's been sixteen very happy years) I still look forward to going to bed just to talk about anything and everything, sometimes for hours.

It's funny how you think you're going to hate something, and it becomes one of the best things you ever did. I guess it's all about keeping an open mind and trying something that initially you're skeptical about. Isn't it nice in life when you are pleasantly surprised?

In addition to meeting Georgina every day for lunch, I tried to involve her in other ways. For example, I shared the mundane things at home, and there were plenty of them. One thing that comes to mind is the way Gabriella believed in giving whoever was changing her a golden shower; which basically meant we changed her at very inopportune times. May I get you some finger sandwiches with that cup of urine? It wasn't the most fun we had in our lives, but we learned to laugh about it.

I also loved the burping time. Gabriella would always return at least a quarter of the bottle down my back. Georgina learned very quickly that when she was fully dressed and ready for work it was **definitely** not the time to burp the baby.

April, 1988
Los Angeles
Dressed To Kill

I remember visiting Georgina's office, not knowing that my back was covered in vomit. Everyone was looking at me as I passed by in the hall. I didn't know until later that I had Gabriella's spit up right down the spine of my shirt. Prior to my discovery I had conned myself into believing that I was looking really good that day. I took the stares as compliments, but I did wonder why the men were looking just as intently as the women.

Time marched on and everything was going pretty well with the process of me morphing into Mr. Mom until Gabriella was about eight months old. Unpleasant feelings started surfacing in me. I felt inadequate as a man. My father was very unhappy with my decision to be a stay-at-home dad, and that, coupled with Georgina's lack of time with Gabriella, plunged me into a deep depression. I guess you could call it the man's version of post-partum blues.

2

CHILDCARE

PATIENCE IS A VIRTUE

PATIENCE IS A VIRTUE,
VIRTUE IS A GRACE,
GRACE IS A LITTLE GIRL
WHO WOULDN'T WASH HER FACE.

November, 1988
Los Angeles
Reality Sets In

As a man, it was amazing how I took childcare for granted. I had no idea how I would really respond to the job. Gabriella was one of the most important parts of my life, but I found out through practical experience that this career was not ego-driven, but rather, emotionally driven. I did not get the respect of my peers for doing this type of job because I produced no tangible "product" or "income" with which others could readily identify.

There was no instant gratification. I never heard one of my male friends say to me, "Wow man, you're doing a phenomenal job with those kids! The way you closed that diaper deal, now that was classic." I began to understand why women wanted to enter the work place. Other than those doing it, and hopefully the kids, nobody really values the job. Also, the one who is parenting is usually made to feel that he or she is not a productive part of society.

Although I had Georgina's support in continuing to be Mr. Mom, I was finding it harder to live with myself. At that point in time, I seriously considered going back to work and leaving Gabriella with a nanny, until an unsettling event changed my mind.

Late November, 1988
Los Angeles
Are You Talking To Me

Gabriella, Georgina and I used to live in a townhouse that was next door to a couple that we had befriended. Their names were Harry and Hallie. Hallie was about five feet four inches tall, slender, with brown hair, but she wore a lot of pancake makeup to hide a bad post-acne problem that was probably a remnant of her teenage years.

Harry, about five feet nine inches tall, with brown hair (slightly balding), constantly had a pained look on his face. At first I thought Harry's look was the way he was born, but later I realized that it was how he viewed life. He was not a happy man. He was extremely pessimistic. They used to call each other "lovey" like the Howells on *Gilligan's Island*. A couple of times I almost slipped and called him "Thurston" instead of Harry.

We each had a three-story townhouse that was joined by a common wall. Harry and Hallie had a little girl named Melissa, whom they called Missy for short. Missy was about eight months younger than Gabriella. Missy appeared to be a bright and happy baby. Harry worked and Hallie stayed home most of the time, but she did work a couple of nights a week. They were both psychotherapists who were also in therapy themselves. I always wondered about that. When you go to a therapist who is in therapy themselves, is it like getting a constant second opinion? I guess that's a whole other issue to ponder.

Missy would often come over to our house to play with Gabriella. Since we lived next door and our children enjoyed playing together, we became very friendly with Harry and Hallie. One day Hallie called and told me that she and Harry needed some time alone. They decided to hire a Mexican woman as a baby sitter who was recommended by their Dominican Republic cleaning lady, who was originally recommended by the El Salvadoran cleaning lady of another friend of theirs, who was, in turn recommended by the Honduran baby sitter of that friend's neighbor. And if that doesn't tie you into knots, try this: Peter Piper picked a peck of pickled peppers, peckers pick a peck of pickles, Peter. Oh, forget it!

This was the first time they had ever left Missy with someone other than family. Hallie asked if Georgina and I would be home that night, and if we would listen for anything unusual. I actually found that very funny. What did they want us to do? Listen at the common wall with a glass? I offered to have Missy stay with us, but Hallie didn't want to impose and I didn't push the issue. She was satisfied with her choice and who was I to make waves?

As soon as they left, I heard Missy starting to cry. She went on crying and crying. Thirty minutes had passed and I was about to call the number that Hallie had left us in case of an emergency, when our phone rang and it was Hallie. She asked me if I would go over to their place and see if everything was okay. They had tried calling and nobody answered the phone.

I started to panic; a strange person was over at their home and this little girl had not stopped crying for half an hour. At this point I was conjuring up all kinds of things that could be happening to this kid. I raced over to their house and started banging on the door. "Open this door right now!" I shouted. The baby sitter opened the door and stood there with a very frightened look on her face. Missy was on the floor with toys around her crying "Mommy left!" Obviously, she was all right; just very upset at being left with a stranger. I couldn't talk to the woman because as I quickly realized, she didn't speak any English and I was not able to converse in Spanish. In fact, her inability to speak English was the reason she didn't answer the telephone in the first place.

I'm not trying to cast any aspersions on foreigners that don't speak English who are taking care of kids of a strictly English speaking family, but as Strother Martin said to Paul Newman in the movie *Cool Hand Luke*, "What we have here is a failure to communicate."

I think that event woke me up. It was as if someone had slapped me in the face and said, "Mark, why do you give a damn about what other people think? Stop this self pity, do the job and do it well."

Like Missy, Gabriella's feelings and psyche were at stake. Who would be better to guide her but me? Maybe I would make mistakes, but at least they would be my mistakes. I decided that Mr. Mom would become my career and I would do everything to succeed in it. I also decided something else at that time. I would learn not only from my mistakes, but also from the mistakes of other people.

So what did I learn from Missy's mishap? Maybe that Hallie and Harry exercised bad judgment in screening childcare workers? Aside from that obvious lesson, I also learned that if I were to leave Gabriella with anyone, a trial period with the sitter while I was at home would probably help make both of us feel more comfortable.

As I thought deeper about child rearing, a question came to mind. Who is really doing this job? I observed three types of parents. One, there were the committed moms or dads who spent a lot of time with their children. These parents gave their children time for learning and play, provided emotional support, and were physically present, whether it was during the middle of the night, or through whatever situations the child may have needed help with.

Two, there were the moms and dads who would have liked to personally take care of their children, but who had financial obligations which forced both parents to work. These parents, however, still tried to be there as much as they could and made all other activities secondary to their children. Lastly, there were the part-time moms or dads who wanted to delude themselves into believing they were there for their children but needed "for their sanity," a lot of alone time. These parents regularly left their children in the care of others.

I sincerely felt that taking care of my children was the most important job that I could do and that it would demand all of my time for me to be truly successful. I compared it to anyone who intended to become very successful in any business or career.

You always hear of such a person being described as a workaholic; slaving at the office day and night, meticulously making sure the job is done correctly. The reason for expending that level of effort is simple to understand; that is what is required to succeed. I decided that if I wanted to succeed in the raising of my children, then it would require that same level of effort. It was a full-time job that would demand my constant and painstaking input.

It now became very apparent to me that when Georgina and I decided to have Gabriella, it basically changed our lives forever. We were not free to do the things that we did before, when it was just the two of us. Sometimes, that is a hard concept for any parent to grasp. You sometimes try to do anything you can to regain some of the freedoms that you once had, attempting to relieve yourself from the responsibility of being a parent. That's not to say that it isn't okay to take some time for yourself or your marriage once in a while, but I was under no delusions—having a child was a big, serious, mature step in life.

When we decided to take that plunge and become a mother and father, we felt compelled to devote the effort and the time we believed our child deserved. I learned early on that Gabriella was worth every second that I could give her. The more I gave, the more I got, and the more I got, the more I wanted to give. I realized then that, as parents, if we would continue that circle for our family, we could create our own little paradise: a Garden of Eden right here on Earth.

3

LET'S HAVE A PARTY

COME OUT TO PLAY

BOYS AND GIRLS, COME OUT TO PLAY;
THE MOON DOES SHINE AS BRIGHT AS DAY.
LEAVE YOUR SUPPER AND LEAVE YOUR SLEEP,
AND COME WITH YOUR PLAYFELLOWS INTO THE STREET.
COME WITH A WHOOP, COME WITH A CALL,
COME WITH A GOOD WILL OR COME NOT AT ALL.

December, 1988
Los Angeles
Party Planning

As the first year of being Mr. Mom came to a close, Georgina and I prepared for Gabriella's birthday party. This was, of course, a monumental event for the parents of a one-year-old. Personally, I don't think Gabriella really cared who was at her party or, for that matter, whether she had a party at all. But as parents of a first (and, at the time only) child, Gabriella's birthday made for a very important celebration.

Before our daughter's party arrived, we were invited to another child's first birthday party. The birthday girl was the daughter of a friend of Georgina's who lived in Malibu, California. This gave us a chance to see to what lengths other parents would go with a first birthday.

December, 1988
Malibu, California
Life's a Beach

There were very detailed instructions on how to get to the party. The home was in one of Malibu's exclusive residential canyons, apparently right near Barbara Streisand's compound. As we drove down the road towards the house, I could already hear the echo of the song *"People"* ringing off the surrounding five-plus acre estates. I remember thinking that although it might be true that people who need people are the luckiest people in the world, with the trek it would take them to get to each other's homes, how lucky could they really be?

We arrived at the party and, as expected, found that they had held nothing back. The grounds were decorated like a Rio carnival. Colorful paper lanterns were strung from the trees. Mariachi music was playing and there was a huge piñata hanging in the center of the yard. Up on a hill there was a large landing where there were pony rides.

After saying our hellos to the parents, we made the climb up to where the ponies were. Gabriella was pretty adventurous and seemed excited to have a ride. There was only one pony so we had to wait our turn, but the birthday girl wouldn't get off to give another child a chance to ride. The mother was summoned up on the hill to deal with the problem. She arrived with the nanny and forcefully took her child off the pony. The birthday girl was screaming and had a complete fit. After the mother took her from the horse, she handed the little girl right over to the nanny, who whisked her off toward the house.

The mother was apologizing for her daughter's behavior, saying that the child was tired and not to let this deter us from continuing to have a good time.

The birthday girl was not heard from again until the time for birthday cake. She didn't seem very happy. I wonder what that little girl was wishing for when she blew out those candles. Happy birthday! As far as the incident with the pony went, maybe her daughter was tired, but if that was typical of how much comfort I received from my mother, I would be tired too. I really felt sorry for the birthday girl. There was no discussion or even the least bit of coaxing to get her off that pony. I realized that whatever we decided to do for Gabriella's birthday would be fine as long as we were there with our hearts open and we enjoyed the party as a family.

After that party some thoughts came to mind about kids' parties in general. I wondered again if Gabriella really wanted a party. Do you think a one-year-old or two-year-old really cares about any party? Give a child that young the leftover box from any package, and he or she becomes the happiest and busiest little child in the world. There was a time in my life when a party was the **last** thing I wanted.

July, 1964
Toronto, Canada
What If You Threw A Party And No One Came?

I remember when I was turning six years old. We had moved to a new neighborhood about a year before and I had just started a different local school that was down the block from my house. The previous year we were bussed to another school, while the local school was being built. I had no friends but I liked it that way. I was fairly antisocial at the time.

My mother wanted to have a party for my sixth birthday at our new house. She made up about twenty invitations and told me to hand them out in school to all my classmates. Needless to say, being as antisocial as I was, a party wasn't my idea of a good time. My mother didn't want to hear my voice of discontent; she basically forced me to invite everyone in the class.

I remember going to school with a sinking, gut-wrenching feeling, wondering how I was going to hand out twenty invitations, one by one. I started out by cautiously giving the first invitation to a kid named Alan. I gave him his invitation in the schoolyard, making sure there was a teacher present. I had a good reason for this precaution. Three days before he and his friend had jumped me after school and tried to beat me senseless. Luckily, the same teacher was passing by and broke it up before I was seriously hurt. I didn't give it too much thought at the time, but I can imagine what that teacher must have been thinking about me inviting that bully to my party.

Next, I gave an invitation to a boy named Joe. I would try to stay real clear of him. Joe was a very scary kid. He had a tattoo by the time he was five years old and it wasn't one of those temporary ones either. He told us his father said that it would make him stronger; that he would become a real man. He was always punching walls in school to prove his manhood. I can only speculate where this kid is today. If there were any justice, he would be impersonating the construction worker in a *Village People* touring band. Can you imagine how proud his father would be of that macho man? I gave those two invitations out first because I wanted to get the safety issue over and done with.

When I gave the girls their invitations, they just looked at me like I was a quivering pile of protoplasm, with LOSER written all over me. "Who is this geek, and why is he inviting us to his party?" It was a humiliating experience. There was tremendous relief after I gave out all the invitations and I could return to the safety of my antisocial behavior.

During the next couple of weeks, there was a lot of party-related activity going on. My mother and siblings were making games, party favors and buying all the things to create what would be, I was assured, the best party ever.

The day of the party came all too soon. I woke up in the morning and I have to admit, I was lulled into a false sense of security by how good everything looked. The decorations were beautiful. Streamers laced the room and a huge pin-the-tail-on-the-donkey was plastered up on the wall. Now maybe some of you don't think that a gigantic pin-the-tail-on-the-donkey is much by today's standards, but in 1964 that big ass, sprawled across the wall, was pretty impressive to me.

The party was scheduled to start at 11:00 in the morning. We all waited with great anticipation. The clock struck eleven, then eleven fifteen, then eleven thirty, but no one showed up except a neighbor who lived in another house behind us. His mother dragged him over, like a cat would drag in its prey, ready for the slaughter. His parents were friends with my parents, which explains why he was forced to come to my party. My mother asked me whether I was sure that I had given out the invitations. I replied defensively, "Yes."

I really wasn't upset that nobody came to my party. I was actually quite relieved. I didn't like those kids; they weren't my friends and the last thing I wanted was to have a party with them. But then came the worst part of the whole experience. My parents and my siblings stared at me with their sorrowful eyes. They felt so bad for me, that it started to make me feel bad.

To make matters worse, my mother thought that I was so upset, she made the neighbor's son stay and play all the games with me that she and my siblings had created. Of course, he won all the prizes. At the time, I was actually hoping that hide-and-seek was one of the party games, because I was constantly looking for the nearest rock to crawl under.

I know my mother tried to do her best by giving me a party, but if she had known who I was at the time, she would have realized that forcing a party on me was a blueprint for disaster. I appreciate her intentions in trying to get me to develop friendships, but she had to let me do that on my own, and for me it had to be done slowly, one friend at a time.

I am aware that her heart was in the right place although her actions were a little misguided. Sometimes it's hard to know what the right decision might be for any given situation. We all try to do our best, but one thing I learned from that experience is, as a parent, to be careful and to look before I leap.

January, 1989
Malibu, California
Back to the Beach

We decided to have a party for Gabriella, but just a small one in our townhouse with family members and a few friends. Georgina and I wanted to get Gabriella a nice present that she would enjoy, so we bought her a large stuffed bear. We also felt that a more educational toy would be appropriate, so we were on the search for something unique and felt that her direct input would be required.

Georgina knew a very prominent record producer and his wife. They were renting a house in the Malibu colony directly on the beach in Malibu, California. They were having their multi-million dollar dream house built on the opposite side of the Pacific Coast Highway in the same area. This is an area in Southern California where a number of the movie stars and very wealthy people live. The producer's wife invited Georgina to a Tupperware party at their house on the beach.

The party involved Tupperware for kids; a line of kid's toys that is sold by Tupperware. You were asked to bring your child and pick out some toys for him or her. At the time, I thought it was very strange for someone of that stature and financial success in business to have a Tupperware party. Upon reflection, I realized that given the "plastic nature" of so many Hollywood people it complemented their behavior.

When Georgina got to the Malibu party she knocked on the door and a maid answered. She went into the house with Gabriella. When Georgina walked in, she saw several women looking at toys but there were no children. The door maid told her to leave Gabriella in the other room with her nanny. Since we didn't have a nanny, Georgina informed them that she would keep Gabriella with her; after all, she was there to buy toys for Gabriella and it would be nice to have her opinion on what she liked and didn't like.

Out of curiosity, Georgina opened the door to the other room where the children were. She told me that there were about twelve maids in the room, sitting on chairs facing each other in two straight lines with twelve little kids on their laps. Now that I think of it, maybe they were reenacting the children's book *Madeline*. Twelve little maids with twelve little kids in straight lines and the smallest maid was named Rosa? On second thought, I don't think it works as well as the original.

Georgina told me that the mothers would run into the other room every once in a while to show their kids a toy. Even though you were supposed to bring your child, participation with that child was definitely limited. I wonder what kind of charade these women were playing. Perhaps the children were the "beards" to create an accepted social gathering, or maybe it was some sort of psychic experiment. "Junior,

Mommy is in the other room thinking of a toy; please take that pacifier out of your mouth and concentrate!"

Georgina and Gabriella came home with a shape sorter. It's a toy where you have to put the right shape in the right hole. Not that inventive, but it was uniquely designed and Gabriella liked it. Aside from the hand-eye coordination and dexterity it taught, I think filling holes correctly, whether it's one in your head or one in your heart, is a good lesson to learn early on in life.

We had Gabriella's first birthday party, which completed one of the most rewarding years in my life. I was a Mr. Mom and I had started to enjoy it and would do everything it took to become an expert. I would become a workaholic at my job and create the finest product that the world had ever seen. My career had begun.

4

AND ONE MAKES FOUR

WHISTLE

THERE WERE TWO WRENS UPON A TREE,
WHISTLE AND I'LL COME TO THEE;
ANOTHER CAME, AND THERE WERE THREE,
WHISTLE AND I'LL COME TO THEE;
ANOTHER CAME AND THERE WERE FOUR.
YOU NEEDN'T WHISTLE ANY MORE.

January, 1990
Los Angeles
Sex: Recreation or Procreation?

Another year went by and the job of being Mr. Mom was going along superbly. I had settled into the position and my boss (Gabriella) was happy with me. Productivity and growth was at an all-time high. Georgina, as the production manager, decided that since everything was going along so well, we should create another position for a second boss. Or for that matter, literally create a second boss. Since she believed that in a good company you should always promote from within, the stage was set.

At first I thought it wasn't a bad stage on which to perform, but as Michael Keaton said in the motion picture *BeetleJuice*, after he wore himself out with one spectacular exhibition of his talents, "That's why I won't do two shows a night." Little did I know that it wasn't the two shows that were the problem, it was the on-demand performance that got to me.

I remember when Georgina would call me in a panic from work, saying she was coming right home because the "window of opportunity" was open. I never realized when it came to sex, how little "opportunity" I wanted at that time. As a man, what did I know or care about basal temperature rising? There was only one thing I was taught that had to ascend and during "baby-making time" I barely had that under control. The pressure was almost too much to bear, but Georgina was on a mission, and whether I liked it or not, I was drafted and became a missionary.

We had Gabriella's second birthday party in a local park and it was thoroughly enjoyable. It wasn't a big bash; it was just enough to make it fun. The highlight of the party for Gabriella was when my sister-in-law arrived with her newly adopted puppy. My sister-in-law came late, and as she strutted toward us, my father-in-law announced, "Here comes the Bimbo." Apparently, that was the dog's name.

At first I was a little taken aback and I thought my father-in-law was referring to his daughter. Although he had a pretty good sense of humor and my sister–in-law did dress very provocatively, it still was pretty bizarre, coming from her own father. It didn't take me too long to realize after my sister-in-law got closer to us, that he was referring to the puppy. In keeping with his humor though, he later commented to me in private that he now had two bimbos in the family.

July, 1990
Los Angeles
The Preschool Blues

Georgina became pregnant again. Our family would be growing and adjustments would have to be made. Gabriella would not be the only child anymore. She would have to share the limelight.

I didn't want the experience of having a sibling to be traumatic for Gabriella. I wanted to find a way for her to adjust well to this new situation. I knew this would take a lot of work, but I also knew the time and the effort would definitely be worthwhile.

After talking it over with Georgina we decided to enroll Gabriella in nursery school. She was two and a half years old and because she was our first child, we didn't really know if this was the right time to start her schooling. As there was a new baby on the way and given that most parents that I knew in Los Angeles had palmed off their children since birth, I thought it would be okay. At the moment we made that decision, I didn't realize that Gabriella would have such a terrible time making the transition.

It was a good school and, looking back, they were very helpful about the whole thing, as I ended up breaking new ground there. I couldn't leave Gabriella and let her cry as I walked away. The teacher told me to just go and Gabriella would only cry for a couple of minutes and then she'd be fine. I told her that I couldn't do that and asked to stay for a while. They were not initially very happy about that request and said it would disrupt the class. I told them if they didn't let me stay and do this my own way I would take her out of the school. There is a saying, "Money talks and bullshit walks," but as I found out, if you paid your bill in full, you could bullshit your way through anything. In that situation I was flying by the seat of my pants. I wasn't sure whether my plan would work, but I had to go with my instinct.

Over a period of four months I left the classroom for maybe half an hour at a time, getting Gabriella used to the school and the teachers. Finally, one day I said to her, "Gabriella, can I leave?" She asked me when I would come back to get her. I said, "Whenever you want me to; you just tell the teacher and I will be here." I could see it wasn't easy for her but she let me go.

Those months were very long and hard, but that's what it took for her to feel confident about this new situation in her early life. With other children the process might have been shorter and easier, but with Gabriella I had to take the time to know how she felt about this event, which she viewed as monumental.

To figure out how Gabriella really felt took instinct. Obviously, when she was a baby, she didn't know how to speak; but somehow I knew when she was hungry, tired, had to be changed and so on. I had to ask myself, how did I know all these things? I learned to communicate on what I now call the inner level, the level of feelings.

I promised myself that as she grew and began to speak, I would not forget that level of communication. When Gabriella wouldn't tell me what I needed to know, I would draw on this inner level of connection to try to help her. I would need to somehow decipher the original language of humanity—remember back to when she was a baby and open myself up to the unspoken word. I would have to listen to what I *felt*; because I knew that those feelings were where all truth lies.

February, 1991
Los Angeles
It's A Boy!

Georgina gave birth to our son Daniel at Cedars-Sinai Medical Center in Los Angeles, California. We had a very unique experience with the birth of Daniel. Even though I roomed in with Georgina when Gabriella was born, I didn't think that the hospital would allow Gabriella and I to do the same thing. I decided that I would really push the envelope this time and not only room in with Gabriella but also involve her all the way through the birth of Daniel.

We arrived at the hospital at eight in the evening. Georgina's parents met us there just in case I needed someone to watch Gabriella. I proceeded into the birthing room with Georgina. They conducted the usual tests: ultrasound, fetal monitoring for the baby's heartbeat, and a few more things that doctors do with their hands that would make any husband a little uncomfortable.

After the initial examination they told Georgina that she wasn't quite ready and that she should walk around for a while. I guess the bun wasn't fully baked yet. Unlike an oven, I couldn't just turn her up to four hundred degrees so we could get things rolling. As I knew from Gabriella's birth, nature was in control of the situation and we just had to wait. Gabriella had to wait too and she did. She waited and waited and waited. She paced with her daddy inside and outside the labor room. She waited with me until five o'clock in the morning.

Finally, while Gabriella was in the birthing room, Georgina went into full labor. I quickly took Gabriella out of the room to her grandparents and fifteen minutes later Daniel was born. I immediately took Gabriella in to see her new baby brother. She came into the room, looked at Daniel, kissed him on the cheek and said, "I love you, I waited for you all the night and now I'm tired. Let's all go to sleep."

About thirty minutes later Gabriella, Georgina, Daniel, and I went into Georgina's regular hospital room. There was a single bed and a cot. The nurses helped Georgina into the bed and she went right to sleep. Gabriella and I pushed the cot next to Georgina's bed and we lay down next to her. Daniel was in a bassinet and started whimpering. Gabriella, with half-lidded eyes looked at me and said, "Daddy, what about Daniel?" I went over to Daniel and took him back to the cot. With Gabriella and Georgina on one side, me on the other and Daniel in the middle, our new family had its first night's sleep.

I was hoping even though Gabriella was just three years old, that she would create a bond and a connection with Daniel right away. She did. In her own way Gabriella labored for Daniel as much as her mother and I did. Okay, maybe Georgina labored slightly more than I did, but no man is an island, I felt that this time it was okay to delegate.

5

IT'S NOT A PERFECT WORLD

LADYBIRD, LADYBIRD

LADYBIRD, LADYBIRD,
FLY AWAY HOME,
YOUR HOUSE IS ON FIRE
AND YOUR CHILDREN ALL GONE;
ALL EXCEPT ONE
AND THAT'S LITTLE ANN
AND SHE HAS CREPT UNDER
THE PUDDING PAN.

March, 1992
Los Angeles
"Safety First"

Gabriella and Daniel were getting along beautifully. They had such love for each other. There were times I would just sit there and watch them interact, and wonder what I did so right in this lifetime, to be blessed in this way.

At the same time that I was relishing my children, Los Angeles was getting more and more violent. Crime seemed out of control and there wasn't enough of a police department to combat the criminal element. I remember one day I took Gabriella and Daniel to a park in Marina Del Rey. We didn't live far from there and it was a very good part of town.

We had a nice day in the park and left at about three o'clock in the afternoon. An hour after we came home, I was listening to the radio and in a news bulletin they reported that there was a drive-by shooting in that park about ten minutes after we had left. Although I was thankful that we weren't there at the time of the shooting, I had to wonder, "What about next time?" When Georgina came home that night I told her that I think we should consider moving out of Los Angeles.

April, 1992
Los Angeles
Living Under Marshal Law

Things went from bad to worse and I was becoming more and more uneasy with living in Los Angeles. In April of 1992, after the Rodney King verdict was handed down, riots broke out all over the city. It wasn't only confined to certain areas either. We had a loft in our condo that had a deck from where you could look out and see the skyline of Los Angeles. We stood there in disbelief and watched the smoke rise as the city burned.

That night there were local reports of gangs looting and entering homes. The police were spread so thin that if you needed them, they could not respond. I stayed up all night worrying for my family and feeling helpless to defend them. I had no weapon and two blocks away there were reported problems. Helicopters buzzed over our house with searchlights illuminating the night sky. At around three o'clock in the morning Georgina, Gabriella and Daniel had fallen asleep together on the couch. I just stood there looking at them. They were my life, my heart and my soul. Seeing all their beautiful faces, I started to cry, and for the first time in my life, I wondered whether my luck had truly run out. I sat down and prayed.

The night passed and in the morning the militia arrived. A soldier armed with an AK-47-assault weapon, dressed in full fatigues, stood guard at the market where we shopped. The military enacted a curfew of 9:00 PM for every citizen in the city. I felt like I was living in a war zone. All the televised images of Beirut seemed much closer now. I couldn't believe this was America. Faced with riots, drive-by shootings and earthquakes, I knew it was time to move.

October, 1992
Los Angeles
There Is Light At The End Of The Tunnel

In October of 1992, Georgina received a call from a long-time friend of hers who informed her about a job at a big pharmaceutical company in New Jersey. It was six months after the riots, and Georgina and I were eager to move. She interviewed for the job and was offered the position two days later. After less than two minutes of discussing the new opportunity we accepted the offer.

A month later, we went East to look for a house. The company offered an excellent relocation package. They bought our townhouse in Los Angeles and helped us arrange for a favorable mortgage rate, which enabled us to afford a house in New Jersey. Everything was falling into place. I was back again on my career track. It looked like I was destined to be Mr. Mom, and as I found out later, my work was cut out for me.

6

MY NEW WORLD

ONE FOR THE MONEY

ONE FOR THE MONEY,
AND TWO FOR THE SHOW,
THREE TO GET READY,
AND FOUR TO GO.

December, 1992
New Jersey
Start Spreading the News

When we arrived in New Jersey in December, the first order of business was to freeze our derrières off. The next thing on our list was to get Gabriella adjusted to her new school and settle into the neighborhood. We arrived halfway through the academic year, so I wanted to make sure that Gabriella's transition was as smooth as possible.

I lived in Los Angeles for many years but was no stranger to the East Coast. Growing up in Toronto, Canada and living in New York for eight months after I married Georgina, made me very aware of how unique the atmosphere was here. They had a distinct demeanor, unlike the rest of the country. There was an aggressive edge to them. Most of the time they'll tell you exactly what is on their mind, sometimes to the point of rudeness, but it can be refreshing to know where you stand and not have to guess at people's motives. Actually, I enjoyed the change from Los Angeles. I had a lot of trouble getting friends in Los Angeles to open up to me. They always seemed to be playing a role; they tried very hard not to let you inside. It seemed to me that even in my closest relationships, I was still dealing with a Hollywood façade.

February, 1993
New Jersey
Close Encounter of the Suburban Housewife Kind

I found that being Mr. Mom in the suburbs was very different than being Mr. Mom in a city. I felt very judged when I first came in contact with the women in the neighborhood. Believe it or not, because I was a stay-at-home dad, some of the women here assumed I was in a "marriage of convenience." You know that dark, terrible, suburban secret: the corporate-minded overachieving wife who wanted to have children and the obliging but fundamentally gay husband. Do you have one of those where you live??? So they kept their distance. There was a friendly attitude, but no one wanted to get too close.

In those early days in New Jersey, I certainly learned that I was breaking new ground; I would have to change people's preconceived ideas. I guess men are just not perceived as having the desire, or even the patience, to take care of children and if they do, then something *must* be wrong with them. Socializing with the women in the neighborhood seemed definitely out of the question. I was isolated and found no other adult companionship other than Georgina, and she was working very hard in her new job and didn't have much time to give me.

March, 1993
New Jersey
Baby Number Three

Before I became too lonely, to our surprise, Georgina became pregnant again. We were talking about having another baby, but since she had just started a new job, there were no plans to have another child at that time. She became nervous about what impact maternity leave would have on her relatively new career at the company.

Sometimes as a man, you think that you have timed things perfectly, but nature decides that it has its own agenda, and as a result, you have no choice but to follow the flow.

Georgina's pregnancy stopped her from working so hard. Her work hours were more reasonable until six months into the pregnancy, when she unexpectedly went into early labor and was placed on total bed rest by her doctor.

The days were turning cooler, as the fall went into full swing. Gabriella had started first grade and was adjusting well to her new school. It now became time to place Daniel in preschool, before the new baby was born. Two months before the birth of our third child, I found myself back in a classroom sitting with Daniel, in a repeat performance of the days with Gabriella in Los Angeles. It was much harder for me this time. I had to balance Gabriella's school progression, Daniel's preschool and Georgina's confinement at home, all at the same time. Those were very hard months; but one good thing about my life then was, that because I was so busy, I found that the loneliness that had plagued me earlier in the year had all but disappeared.

January, 1994
New Jersey
And One More Makes Five

Georgina went into labor on January 18 at 3:00 am. Daniel and Gabriella were fast asleep in their rooms. There was a horrific snowstorm outside and, even though I debated not taking Gabriella and Daniel with us to the hospital, the lack of anyone to leave them with really forced my hand.

We loaded up the car and began the twenty-minute ride to the hospital. About ten minutes into the drive, Georgina went into a very severe labor, the kind where you want to call your husband all kinds of names. She held herself back from doing so, until we came to a red traffic light. As a very law-abiding citizen (even in the middle of the night, in a snowstorm without another soul on the road), I felt compelled to stop. After waiting about thirty seconds for the light to change and enduring at least seventeen different types of profanities (luckily the kids had fallen asleep in the back seat), I raced to the hospital.

After we arrived at the hospital, the duration of the labor was very short. Within thirty minutes, Rebecca was born. Gabriella and Daniel were very excited to have their new sister. We stayed in the hospital all day with Georgina and the new baby, but then the time came to leave. Contrary to my experience with Daniel's birth in Los Angeles, where Gabriella and I slept in Georgina's room with the new baby, four people in a small hospital room was even too much for me to ask the nurses to arrange. Although it saddened Georgina, when night fell, Gabriella, Daniel and I went home to sleep.

That night when Georgina was in the hospital with Rebecca, I hardly slept. I felt guilty for not staying with Rebecca. I had remained with the other two and I wanted to give Rebecca the same start in life that I had given Gabriella and Daniel. I missed that first night's bonding that I felt was so important. I drove myself absolutely crazy until I suddenly realized that as a parent I wouldn't be able to do everything that I wanted, but I would strive to do everything that I could. I would make sure that Rebecca would get my message, the continuing message that I tried to give to Gabriella and Daniel. I would be her daddy forever. I would find the way to guide her, send and keep her on the right path in this life. I would love her deep within my heart and would accept her, unconditionally. **I would be there for her**.

August, 1994
New Jersey
New Adjustments

Georgina returned to work six months after Rebecca was born. It seemed to me that to make up for lost time, her company expected that she work harder than ever. While she was at home, the help she gave me with the children was truly a lifesaver. It reinforced to me that the job of taking care of children was definitely a two-person, full-time position, and doing it alone was very difficult. I had new respect for the single parent.

The first month of Georgina's return to work again sent me into a depression. I felt alone and stretched very thin. I was constantly being pulled in three different directions. The job of being Mr. Mom became physically draining. Going through the day-to-day diaper changes, feedings, the never-ending household chores, and looking after my older two all at the same time was exhausting. There was soccer for Gabriella, gym class for Daniel and many other activities that I had to balance. I was so tired at night that I would literally collapse in bed. I think my eyes shut before my head hit the pillow and opened shortly after that when Rebecca or Daniel had a problem in the night. They were never very good sleepers. When Gabriella and Daniel started school in September, things got a little easier, but through all the work and fatigue, I still felt a little isolated.

Did I say a little isolated? I think that at the time, it felt as if I had been put into solitary confinement. I desperately needed some adult contact. I knew I had to reach out and find some friends. The question was, how? I had one friend, Larry, whom I had met while I was coaching Gabriella in soccer. Like every other male in the community, however, he worked during the day. So what was a lonely, weary man to do? With one walk around the block, everything changed.

October, 1994
New Jersey
Nice To Meet You

It was a beautiful autumn day in October and like many other days, while Gabriella and Daniel were in school, I took Rebecca for a walk in her stroller. I was about half way down the street when a woman stopped me. "Hi" she said, "My name is Sue and I live in the neighborhood." Before I could say anything she went on briskly to say, "Some of the girls and I were talking and wondering if you would like to get together with us for lunch tomorrow? You might call it a "getting-to-know-you" lunch. You are fairly new to the area so we thought we should introduce ourselves; please, bring your little girl with you."

How friendly I thought. I accepted the invitation and asked her where and when. Sue said, "At my house. Sixty two Regal Street, about 12:30 p.m." Sue looked a little older than me, but I thought to myself,

"This is a start, maybe some of the women in the neighborhood will finally accept a man into their world." What I didn't know at the time was what a world I was about to enter.

I was very excited about the lunch. I never kept great relationships with my childhood friends. I had some good friendships, but had never made much of an effort to keep in touch and make them strong as an adult. I was determined to change all that. I was ready to make the commitment it would take to have good friends in my life. I was on a mission.

7

You've Got to Have Friends

I LOVE COFFEE

I LOVE COFFEE,
I LOVE TEA,
I LOVE THE GIRLS,
AND THE GIRLS LOVE ME.

October, 1994
New Jersey
Getting To Know You

I arrived at the lunch about five minutes early. To my surprise everyone was already there. It was as if I were the guest of honor. I felt almost presidential as I walked into the kitchen where Sue's friends were sitting. I, of course, mean presidential in the press conference sense, not that I thought in any way that Sue's kitchen was looking like my private oval office. All eyes were on me and I was ready to field any questions.

There were six women at the lunch and Sue very graciously introduced me to them. "Everyone, I would like you to meet Mark from around the corner. He is new to the neighborhood and stays home with his children. He is a **Mr. Mom**." Sue then turned to me and asked me if I would mind her referring to me as Mr. Mom. I told her that would be fine. She then went on with the introduction. "Mark I'd like you to meet (as she pointed to each person) Mary, Amy, Vicky, Julie, and Cathy."

I sat down at the table with Rebecca on my lap. They all started to ask me questions: How and why did I decide to stay at home with my children? How did I feel about the three-thirty bewitching hour? What were meal times like in my house? What did I do to keep my sanity? How did I juggle the hectic schedules of three kids and a working spouse? Did I find it lonely? The question of loneliness seemed to be a common theme. I realized that I wasn't the only one who was feeling the isolation of being a stay-at-home parent.

After the lunch was over, Sue asked me privately, whether I could stay a little longer to speak with her alone. I agreed. As we started talking, Sue very quickly got on the subject of happiness. She told me that she was very unhappy with her husband John. Just at that moment my presidential aura began to slip away and was replaced with an image in my mind of a tuna that was freshly caught in the net of a smiling, warm hearted sushi chef.

Sue started telling me that she was a woman who had come out of the Sixties generation, but, as she put it, was very straight-laced, even a little repressed. She said that I wouldn't believe how that had all changed over the years. I think the beads of sweat started to pour off my forehead. I wanted a close friend, but the Mormon path of many wives was not for me. In a stroke of luck, just minutes before the paramedics were called for the heart attack I was about to suffer, Sue started reminiscing.

She told me that their marriage had started off normally. Nice wedding, everybody lovey dovey, everyone happy. Sue described her husband John as a New Jersey boy, very much into his cars and simple in his tastes. He was bombastic in his behavior, sometimes too loud and obnoxious. But that wasn't the crux of their problem.

As the years went on, John became very successful in his own business. He was a pharmacist and very proud of it. They tried to have kids, but Sue couldn't. She went through hell trying to have a child, but medicine wasn't that advanced in those days so eventually, after many miscarriages, they decided to adopt. Everything went along fine for about six years and then, all hell broke loose.

Sue told me that she started dressing a little provocatively and became quite flirtatious. John, as Sue explained, had a few ideas of his own on that subject. Sue told me that John thought that she was more like his classic car than his wife and he decided that it was time to let some of his friends try "driving" her.

John's friends liked the idea, and because John was nice enough to share, they reciprocated and let John drive their "cars" as well. Sue chuckled and said, "After all, how else would my husband get around, he wasn't going to take public transportation, was he?" At that point I started planning my escape route. Feeling just a little threatened, I picked up Rebecca and started to make a move towards the door. Sue stopped me and said "Please Mark, I know this is a little strange, but give me a chance to explain." I realized then that Sue didn't want me to join her little group. It was as if she wanted to confess her sins to me and see whether I would accept her anyway. I went back to the kitchen and sat down.

Sue told me that she and John started swinging and that she hated him for getting her involved with that lifestyle. It didn't stop there though. After experimenting with swinging for a while, John became bored, so they decided to hang around with nudists. These were not just your garden-variety type nudists; they were swinging nudists. Quite frankly, I never understood that part of the story. I thought that when you're swinging, the idea is to get naked and have sex with other partners. So why the semantic separation between swingers and swinging nudists? Doesn't each group end up naked and have sex anyway? Whether you start off unclothed or end up unclothed seems like a distinction without a difference to me.

Sue continued, telling me that she and John used to frequent many of these nudist parties. At one party Sue told me there was an almost albino white man who came up to her and spoke to her very eloquently. He said that Sue was a beautiful flower that radiated the sun's light. She was impressed with his manner, and was about to tell him so, until she glanced down and noticed that there was a tiepin straight through the middle of his penis. (I guess since the man was Caucasian, it wasn't a black tie event).

Sue then went on to tell me that she was so fixated on the tiepin that all she could say was, "That must have been painful." The man responded with, "Let me tell you how painful it was" and as he was explaining, he started to become aroused. Sue told me that at this point in the conversation she thought it would be a good idea to move on before this person decided to take his tie on the road.

My head was reeling with attempts to keep things straight. Recapping in my mind, I think Sue was now telling me that they had become swinging nudists who were also into masochism? All of a sudden this quiet little suburb to which I had moved had become very noisy, more like a walk on the wild side of *The Valley of the Dolls*.

Carrying around a lot of anger and hurt, Sue told me she eventually exploded. She started, as she put it, really "acting out." Right then I stopped Sue and looked at the time. I had thirty more minutes until Gabriella and Daniel were due home from school and I was hoping it would be enough time for Sue to finish her story. I encouraged Sue to please go on, but quickly, explaining to her that I had to leave soon.

Moving forward, she said that John was continuing to treat her as a possession, but he had a new twist to the scenario. He now also found pleasure in watching. Sue told me she then came to a decision. No, she didn't file for divorce. She didn't like John picking her partners for her anymore, so as a declaration of her independence she was determined to pick her own.

Enter, Club Med. Hedonism vacations. Other lesser well-known hunting grounds. This is when Sue told me she really became the monster John created. Sue recollected that she would go on these vacations and be very promiscuous. One story she recounted to me was about a time when she and John were at Hedonism and Sue decided to try to end John's voyeuristic days. There were two guys, both about twenty-five years old. Sue met these two boys and started to flirt with them. The next thing you know, she took them back to her room and she's doing the dirty deed; the horizontal tango, the double barrel hoe down, (well you get what I mean) having sex with both of them. Sue said that John walked in and became very angry. He did not like what he was seeing. Apparently these men weren't part of his voyeuristic-swinging-nudists-who-were-sometimes-into-masochism-club.

Sue told me that John said to her, as the three of them were going at it, "What are you doing?" Sue replied, "I'll give you one guess." She told me she would have given him the customary three guesses but she was a little preoccupied at the time. Very upset, John just turned around and left.

My time was up; it had been a very enlightening conversation, but I had to leave. When I got to her door, Sue looked at me and said, "I feel that my life is hell and I need a friend." I stood there with Rebecca for a moment and smiled and nodded back at her without judgment and said, "I'll talk to you tomorrow."

November, 1994
New Jersey
Keeping in Touch

Over the next month Sue and I spoke a few times a week. I also kept in touch with her friend Mary, whom I had met at the lunch. I liked Mary. She was a very down-to-earth woman. She was not deep into thinking, but she tapped into a part of life that seemed to elude me. She had me over to her house for coffee one afternoon and we talked extensively about being stay-at-home parents.

Mary told me that she had two children whom she absolutely adored. She seemed so proud and confident that I wondered how she achieved that state of mind. After talking to her for a while she told me that she had not always been the confident and centered person she now was. She told me she had always wanted to play the piano and finally she decided to take lessons. She was very eager to show me how she played. She had only taken lessons for six months and was surprisingly good.

I could see she felt very happy about what she had achieved. I personally didn't view her accomplishment as being something so life changing, but I was happy for her.

Her dream had always been to play the piano. At forty years old, her decision to take piano lessons was her way of finding a part of herself that had laid dormant for years. She had no delusions of playing

Carnegie Hall; she just wanted to play and do something for her self-esteem and enjoyment.

Perhaps I had to grow up a little myself and gain more wisdom. Mary explained to me that she had come to a point in her life where she was going to do something for herself and would pursue a dream that she had never realized. When she had made the decision to stay home with her children, she had forsaken some of her personal desires.

When I came home, very depressing thoughts had entered my mind. Did I give up my dream to become a songwriter and would that decision haunt me for that rest of my life? Gabriella and Daniel were now in school and Rebecca would be there in the blink of an eye. In another moment they would be entering college. Would I be going through the empty nest syndrome? When my children left home, would my days become quiet and vacuous? Would I be feeling a gut-wrenching loss? What should I do now to avoid that situation?

Gabriella, Daniel and Rebecca were really a very significant part of my self-worth and my day-to-day existence, but they will eventually leave or become preoccupied with their own lives and then, what about me?

I took it even one step further. I thought about things right now, in the middle of their upbringing. As much as I love my children, I kept hearing my father's words: *"You're a bum. What are you doing with your life? Do you think that raising your children will provide you with the kind of recognition and self-worth that comes with something you personally achieve?"* Okay, the last sentence was mine. My father talks in broken English and uses short sentences and probably said something like, *"A real man makes money."*

Then I became philosophical. I thought that Society, as a whole, just doesn't recognize the value in what we can accomplish by being dedicated parents. What we do, in staying home with our children, is one of the most selfless jobs to which a person can devote their time. I realized that the long-term rewards of child rearing are not well acknowledged by the majority of the human race.

I knew that I wasn't going to change the world's thinking. The question was, could I change that which was instilled so deeply inside me so that the pain of my children moving on would be eased by the personal accomplishment of raising them? I was not going to solve this question at that time and I knew that it would be an issue that would keep cropping up for years to come.

December, 1994
New Jersey
A Dining Experience, Like No Other

Sue kept asking me whether Georgina and I would go out for dinner with her and John. She wanted me to meet John and felt that a quick bite to eat would be a good way to get acquainted, and see for myself what he was like. I kept questioning whether Sue had ulterior motives or whether she genuinely wanted my friendship and would respect my life style. I talked it over with Georgina and we decided to go out with them.

I was a little neurotic about who would baby-sit for our children. We rarely went out and when we did, we always took the kids with us. Luckily, Georgina's parents were coming into town so we planned the event around the time they would be at our house.

It was a dinner experience that I would never want to repeat. I started to understand why Sue and John had marital problems. In my opinion, the conversational talents that they exhibited as a couple in the restaurant were less then stimulating. We skipped dessert and I was happy that the evening was almost over, but unfortunately there was still the car ride to our house.

On the way home from this fiasco of feasts, while Georgina and I were sitting in the back seat of Sue and John's car, the conversation wound its way around to the making of money (obviously a sore subject for me). John, the pharmacist, started pontificating about what a genius he was for putting pills from a big bottle into a little bottle and making a ton of money doing it.

The food at dinner wasn't good and with John's ego ascending to the heights that it was, the bile from my stomach was starting to creep up, dancing its way with determination until it reached my throat. John then turned to Sue and said, with a sort of lisp, "Just rememberth. Youth ainth nothing without my money honey." Sue had no reply and Georgina and I just felt embarrassed for her.

At that instance, I became very nauseous. I don't know if it was because of the food I had just eaten, John's last statement or because I was feeling under the weather that night, but as we were approaching my house, I couldn't hold it back anymore and vomited all over John's new Mercedes. Georgina apologized to Sue and John and then she helped me into our house. Once there I felt much better and started to laugh. It seemed to me at the time that although we all skipped what most people would consider the best part of the meal, because of my sudden illness, at least John ended up getting his just desserts.

8

IT'S PARTY TIME

A TIME TO CELEBRATE

STAR LIGHT, STAR BRIGHT,
FIRST STAR I SEE TONIGHT,
I WISH I MAY, I WISH I MIGHT,
HAVE THE WISH I WISH TONIGHT.

January, 1995
New Jersey
Party, Party, Party

Between the middle of January and the middle of February it became what Georgina and I liked to refer to as "birthday madness." Three children born within a month of each other meant making three parties in a short span of time. It was a harrowing experience. The parties became more and more elaborate with everyone trying to outdo the rest with an original concept.

Aside from the party, there was also a tremendous emphasis put on the "goody bag"—you know, the party favor that you give each child after the bash to thank him or her for coming. Unfortunately for me, Georgina really got caught up in this. She actually would have goody bag envy. The goody bag was kind of like a status symbol; the better your goody bag was, the more respected you were. "Wow, what a goody bag. Between that and her Lexus, they must really be doing well."

You could be without a mortgage on your house, have a million dollars in the bank, but heaven forbid if that goody bag was substandard— you weren't worth the excrement that a shrimp expels in one day. I did have a thought though: I am hoping if this goody bag competition escalates that some *nouveau riche* family in the area decides to top everyone else and give out funds for college tuition. I just have to make sure that no one expects me to reciprocate.

There was a lot of pressure associated with the birthdays of Gabriella, Daniel and Rebecca, but this particular year on Rebecca's first birthday, I received a tremendous gift. It was a phone call that I'll never forget and that brings me pleasure every day of my life.

My father had a terrible time accepting my decision to stay home and raise my children as my life's work. He was angry with me for years, which stopped us from having any type of meaningful relationship. Although it hurt me deeply, I really didn't blame him. After World War II, he learned the trade of watch repairing and arrived in Canada with nothing more than the shirt on his back. He worked for thirty years in a jewelry store providing for his family. He was from the old school in which a man was the one that worked and it didn't matter if he liked the job or not; he did it anyway because it was his responsibility.

On January 18, 1995 my father called. After wishing Rebecca a happy birthday, he asked to speak to me. I remember the conversation like it was yesterday. He had told me that he had received a letter from Georgina in October of the previous year. In that four months he had read that letter over and over again. He said he wanted to read me the letter:

"Dear Dad,

Mark has struggled painfully with feelings of inadequacy as a son and that he has failed you. He feels that he is not the "man" that you wanted him to be and that he has let you down by not being a provider. I wanted you to see from my (outsiders in a way) perspective that you should be proud of your son as a success not a failure. Although he may not have made the financial success that you dreamed of for him, in the ultimately important qualities such as hard-work, values and strength, you have raised an unqualified success.

Please dad, try to see the man in Mark, because it takes a real man to do what he has chosen to do by raising our three children.

I love you, Georgina."

My father started to cry on the phone. He told me that he has the highest respect for me and that I should continue being a Mr. Mom. He told me that he had given the matter a lot of thought and he had realized that what I'm doing with my life is probably the most important thing anyone can do. "You are molding the future of the world," he said.

I had tears rolling down my face. I could hardly talk. I was stunned. I already held my father in the highest regard, but at that moment words couldn't explain the giant that I was listening to on the other end of that line. This man, who had come from a different generation, and had been taught to view life contrary to the way I was living it, had extended his whole range of thinking. In my eyes he was truly a great man. What also came to mind, was that I couldn't believe Georgina took it upon herself to write such a letter. She had a big heart when it came to doing something that she thought would make me happy.

Now that I had gained my father's respect for my decision to "work" at home, and raise my children, could I undo years of feeling low self-worth, because deep inside I believed that a "real" man was someone who provided financially for his family? As a stay-at-home parent, I knew that to society, I was still invisible. I was not really considered a productive person. Maybe now, with the burden of my father's anger and lack of acceptance being lifted from my shoulders, when I looked in the mirror, I would, for the first time, see a visible, successful "real" man.

9

SEX, LIES AND ROBBERY

HUMPTY DUMPTY

HUMPTY DUMPTY SAT ON A WALL,
HUMPTY DUMPTY HAD A GREAT FALL.
ALL THE KING'S HORSES,
AND ALL THE KING'S MEN,
COULDN'T PUT HUMPTY TOGETHER AGAIN.

April, 1995
New Jersey
The Insiders Club

The parties were over and the winter was behind us. There was spring and soccer season in the air. I was coaching Gabriella's team for the spring soccer session and needed a team mother. Her name was Rachel. I chose her by default. No one else wanted the job. She seemed very nice and was very interested that I was a Mr. Mom. Outside of soccer, Rachel and I became very friendly and before I knew it, I was invited to "Mommy and Me" playgroups with Rebecca.

These playgroups really expanded my social life. I had a chance to meet many more women in the neighborhood and got to know them quite well. The women and I would have playgroup luncheons once every two weeks. We would take turns, preparing lunch for each other, at our respective homes.

The first time I attended one of these lunches, the women were a little apprehensive in talking freely while I was there. I was considered the guy in a girl's locker room. They decided to break the ice when my friend Rachel, who introduced me, made it clear to the other women that I was "cool" and wouldn't divulge the information I obtained from the secret order of suburban women.

June, 1995
New Jersey
Will You Tell The Truth And Nothing But The Truth?

All of the women in the group, with really no exception, had talked extensively about their thinking on different types of sexual behaviors. The first time I ever heard them talk like this, amongst themselves, it came as a complete shock to me. I was attending one of the luncheons with the women, their children who were between one and two years old at the time, and my almost eighteen month old daughter Rebecca.

There was a younger woman there named Carla. She was the mother of one and divorced. She told me she was 25 years old. That was significant, since the rest of us were bordering on forty and all claimed to be happily married. She was dating, so the other women were very interested in living vicariously through her.

She started by telling a story about her and a local single guy who was supposedly the town's "catch." He was a man who owned a local delicatessen and apparently the women regarded him as the most eligible bachelor in our community. This was all news to me; I guess I wasn't up on the latest bachelor-rating chart.

He seemed like he was a very nice guy and had a successful business. I go there myself to buy pickles because he has the best in town, but after hearing Carla's story my hankering for dill has since diminished. The fact that the pickle man had a successful business was very important to Carla. She kept going on and on about how she wanted a big house and a man who would take care of her in style.

In her quest to become a blushing bride again, Carla was very rigid about her criteria. Do you think the phrase "gold digger" might be an appropriate description? If memory serves me correctly though, the pickle man had a bigger problem than the size of his bank account.

The way I heard it, he was not that proficient as a kisser. As Carla told us in gruesome detail, when he kissed her, an image of the polar ice caps melting came to mind. When I inquired as to what exactly that meant, she explained to me that a bucket strapped to her chin wouldn't have sufficed. Needless to say, that romance did not last very long.

Everyone chimed in with many tales of similar experiences and what the women thought of the pickle man and a host of different people in town and nationwide. Even more fascinating than those discussions, was another conversation that occurred at the end of our luncheon. As I was walking out the front door of the house with Rebecca, my friend Rachel, who was talking to her friend Lydia, called me over.

Lydia looked a little embarrassed but her uneasiness didn't squelch her curiosity. She asked me: "Since your situation is reversed, (she meant my staying at home and Georgina working) do you (she kind of hesitated a little) have sex with your wife to get things that you want?"

This blew my mind. As a man, I suspected that women did this, but to freely admit it, especially to me, now that was bold! I felt at that very moment I had then **and only then** entered the inner circle of women and I was honored. My answer was clear: I told her that if I wanted to buy something, Georgina and I would first discuss it and if it were feasible, financially speaking, we would agree to buy it.

I asked Lydia, "How can you have sex with your husband if you really don't want to?" Rachel and Lydia looked at each other and laughed at how naive I really was. Rachel turned to me and said, "After this conversation, I have no doubt. It's confirmed; you truly are a man. You have a lot to learn about how women survive with their husbands in this world."

After talking to each of the women more about the subject of sex, I learned other little tidbits about what they had to deal with in that department. Lydia told me that she has been awakened many times in the middle of the night for sex, with a specific request attached to it. "Just sex and only sex please." At least her husband doesn't forget his manners.

She went on to say that most of the time she felt obligated to give in because she believed it was her duty as a wife. I thought to myself that having sex in that manner constituted robbery on two fronts: First, she was being robbed of her sleep, and second, she was being robbed emotionally.

I said to Lydia: "Why have sex if your heart isn't in it? You are a wife, not a prostitute." That's when I started treading on thin ice. I had allowed myself to become involved with a very intimate part of someone's life, but I couldn't help myself. I thought it was an injustice and I was still idealistic.

Lydia agreed with me and told me that from now on, "No" would become a bigger part of her vocabulary. I was feeling upbeat that she had taken my advice until a fear came over me. What if her husband found out where her new thinking came from? He might get a tad angry with me. I went home to think about what kind of advice I should be giving people and, for that matter, whether I should be giving any at all. Enemies, I didn't need.

I thought a lot about what Lydia had told me. I understood why some women felt obligated to have sex with their husbands when they didn't really want to, but what I didn't understand was why did we as men want to settle for one piece, when we could have the whole pie. Why were we so driven physically, with only the hint of an emotional awareness? I've heard the testosterone argument, but there must be a way that we men can incorporate that drive into a more rewarding experience for ourselves and our partners.

I started to view sex in a totally different way. Yes, it's pleasurable, but there must be other pleasures besides physical ones that sex produces. I wondered *"Is there a way to truly join with each other? Not just physically, but with our souls? A method to create a union that is of one mind, of one essence and of one being? How can I put my single, lonely self aside for a moment and achieve wholeness?"*

I guess one of the obstacles in the way of obtaining this type of experience is that most of us men have never been taught how to free up our feelings. In fact, I was taught just the opposite. In the past, when it came to sex, (no pun intended) I was much more "conquest" and "result" oriented and derived most of the pleasure physically.

But I learned over the years from my marriage that women have a better idea of how to raise their level of passion and consciousness to a point of emotional and spiritual orgasm. I guess you could call it the thinking person's orgasm. Getting right inside each other's minds and hearts to bring about a state that only humans can obtain.

That night Georgina and I discussed how we had accomplished that kind of joining. She said: "Communication. Talking a lot, not just at bedtime but throughout the day and trying to think about each other's needs. A thank you for cleaning out the dishwasher—a little bit of help with the children at bedtime. The importance of never taking each other for granted. Creating warmth by mutually respecting each other."

I told her, "These are good concepts, but what about when you are married for many years? The passion in lovemaking is not the same as it was when you first met. That's not to say it can't be good, but the height of excitement is lessened." Okay, the word lessened is a kind way of saying that physically on a scale of one to ten, sometimes you're struggling to make a five.

I went on to say, "Like everyone else, haven't we experienced times when we go though lull periods, where sex becomes completely unimportant? What does a man do then, other than busying himself with home improvement projects?"

I regretted that last comment. Never tell a woman that you have lull periods, even if it's true. I spent the better part of that evening backtracking; talking extensively about the life that we had made together, reveling in the happiness that our children had brought us and trying to forget what a big mouth I sometimes have. Although communication is very important to create the connection you need together, I learned a lesson that evening that some things are better left unsaid.

When Georgina and I were in bed that night, I tried to deepen the conversation not just by saying, "I love you", but by really looking at her and allowing my innermost feelings to emerge. I found that my emotions soared. A physical response naturally followed, but the difference was that it was based solely on an emotional grounding, which created something very special, the release of the spirit.

With the word spirit I mean an energy that was within me, a sort of electricity. At that point I took my time making love rather than concentrating on the end result and I found that there was another side of me which attempted to join too. I believe that this kind of union might be the higher level of lovemaking; the very thing that we all search for.

I am not suggesting that there wasn't room in our marriage anymore for some good old-fashioned lust. Lust is a very inviting emotion. In fact it had worked for Sue for many years. I just knew that I would try to add the spiritual part once in a while, because I had found something else about intimacy that I truly enjoyed, and how could I go wrong with that?

I realized that it took me a long time to understand certain things that would enrich my life, but once I understood those things, the beauty of it was that now, I would try to pass it along to my children. My hope was that through teaching them the lessons I had learned, maybe I could relieve some of the difficulties they might have in their lives.

I knew that knowledge and experience were very precious commodities in this world. These would be the greatest gifts I could give my children. If I took the time to teach Gabriella, Daniel and Rebecca what I had learned, then I will have given them a chance to go on and learn more than I knew. My task would be to try and create a learning environment so that they would not feel the need to repeat the road that I have already taken. The airplane that the Wright Brothers invented did not need to be reinvented, it just needed to be improved upon. Maybe Gabriella, Daniel and Rebecca could improve on whatever buildings I might build and construct bigger and better ones for themselves.

10

GOOD HELP IS HARD TO FINE

LITTLE BOY BLUE!

LITTLE BOY BLUE,
COME BLOW YOUR HORN!
THE SHEEP'S IN THE MEADOW,
THE COW'S IN THE CORN.
WHAT! THIS IS THE WAY
YOU MIND YOUR SHEEP?
UNDER THE HAYSTACK,
FAST ASLEEP?

September, 1995
New Jersey
Carpool

The summer of 1995 passed uneventfully. I didn't send the children to camp. Gabriella and Daniel went to a private school and money was tight. Daniel entered Pre-Kindergarten and with that I made another new friend. Her name was Angela, and Daniel was good friends with her son. Angela turned out to be a big help to me.

With one-and-one-half year old Rebecca in the mix, it got to a point where running around from place to place, the gymnastics classes, soccer games, birthday parties, play dates, times three got completely out of hand. The first half of that school year was almost unbearable. Feeling exhausted, buried, and burnt out, I was saved when I finally agreed to accept some help. I was very insecure and mistrusting about who I would let help me. I had to know them very well and trust them implicitly. For some reason, I knew I could trust Angela. She seemed down to earth and unpretentious.

January, 1996
New Jersey
Help Is On The Way

My biggest problem was carpool. I hated waking Rebecca up early when it was my day to drive. She was very cranky when I woke her up from her morning beauty sleep. Angela was a very big help in those days. I would call Angela in the morning if Rebecca was still sleeping and she would come over and stay with Rebecca until I returned home. The best thing about it was that Rebecca loved Angela, so there was no problem if she woke up before I returned.

I carpooled with two mothers from the school. Carpooling was very convenient. It kept the costs down (we didn't have to pay for the bus), and I didn't have to drive the kids to school every day. However, it wasn't without its problems. One of the women, Marla, had three children and was a real piece of work. Marla was about five foot two inches tall with blond hair and an elitist air about her. In March, things got a little tense between us.

March, 1996
New Jersey
Maid to Order

I picked up Marla's kids from school and it seemed like a normal day until it came to dropping them off. When I arrived at her house, I did my usual and honked the horn, but no one came to the door. After several honks and a ringing of the doorbell, I came to the conclusion that there was no one home.

I saw that her kids were getting pretty upset, so I explained to them that they shouldn't worry. I would take them back to my house and we would leave a message for their mother on her answering machine. I also told them that I was sure their mother was just a little delayed and would be home soon. I then brought her three children over to my house. In about half an hour Marla called. She was noticeably stressed on the phone.

She asked me, "Do you have my children?" Since it was my turn to pick them up from school, and I had left a clear message that they were at my house, I was wondering if it was a rhetorical question. Just to make absolutely sure, I replied, "Didn't you get my message?" I didn't understand her next response which was, "No, I wasn't sure if the answering machine was there. As soon as I got in, I called you." She then muttered something else. At that moment, I wasn't about to try and figure out what was going on. I told her that her children were at my house and there was no problem. She could come and pick them up.

I then told her kids that their mother had called and she would be coming to pick them up in a few minutes.

When Marla arrived at my house, I thought she had gone completely mad. She was sweating profusely (not a pretty sight) and talking like she was on speed. She started to tell me her tale of woe. Their nanny was supposed to have been there when the kids came home but she had decided to quit in a very abrupt way.

Marla went on to tell me that when she came home she had found the nanny's room cleaned out. Aside from the nanny taking her own belongings, she decided to help herself to a few other things that didn't, in the legal sense, belong to her. Now I understood why Marla had made the comment about the answering machine. I expressed my concern about her unfortunate turn of events. I told her that bringing her children to my house was no problem at all and that I hoped things worked out for her. But to paraphrase Looney Tunes, "That's **not** all folks."

The next day, my not-so-trusty-minivan wouldn't start. After getting it to the mechanic's shop, I was told it would take two days to get replacement parts. I phoned Marla (with the now "milk carton-maid") and asked her if she could switch driving days with me until my van was fixed.

Marla was absolutely frantic on the phone. She told me she couldn't switch car pool days with me because, and I quote, "You don't understand, my help left and I am all alone here. I have to do EVERY-THING." I said three words to her, "Join the club." I ended up getting a loaner car and driving the car pool myself.

That day, when I brought Marla's kids home, there was a huge heavyset woman crammed in the doorway. I could see that entering the house was not going to be an easy feat. She looked like Mama Cass with a bad attitude. Maybe all this woman needed was a ham sandwich to brighten up her day, and I'm sure the kids would have loved to give her one. I'll never forget the look on Marla's kids' faces; obviously they had not had the pleasure of meeting this new nanny yet.

To say they were reluctant to get out of the car is putting it mildly. My heart really went out to those children on that day. Gabriella said to me, "Daddy, is that the new nanny they hired?" I replied "Yes sweetheart and if you're not nice to me, I'm sure I can hire her sister." Gabriella paused for a moment and said "No way! I'll run away from home first before I'll spend one day with her OR her sister." I thought about Gabriella's comment. I wondered whether Marla's children were thinking the same thing.

On the way home, I felt very nervous inside. Tears came to my eyes. What had just happened to Marla's children jarred a memory in me that I must have buried for years.

October, 1967
Toronto, Canada
My Horror Story

I was about nine years old. My parents went on a week's vacation and left my brother, sister and me at home. They hired a person from a childcare employment agency to stay with us. She was a Scottish woman.

Before I continue, let me try to be a little politically correct. As you may have surmised, the story is not going to be a good one. Just because what happened to me involved a Scottish woman doesn't mean I am vilifying all Scottish people. Before I go on with my story, let me say that I enjoy a pint of Guinness as much as the next guy and I love the sound of bagpipes in the morning. Okay, that's enough of that; I think you get my point.

The sitter came with excellent references. To cut to the chase, she absolutely beat the crap out of us. I remember her chasing me up the stairs of our house to the bathroom. I knew she was going to hit me so I locked myself inside and wouldn't open the door.

Outside the bathroom, in a most reassuring voice, she told me to open the door because all she wanted to do was talk about the reason why I wouldn't eat my peas during dinner. I fell for it. I let her in and she slapped me so hard across the face that my cheek instantly swelled up like an infection that has been left unattended, hot and painful. I was crying, but I knew no one would come to my aid.

She was a bitter, horrible old woman. She told my brother, sisters and me that if we said anything to our parents that she would be back. Believe me that was the last thing I wanted. I was petrified to utter a word about anything.

When my parents returned I kept my mouth shut but my older brother didn't. Once he started telling them what happened, we all chimed in. The worst part of the whole experience wasn't getting hit myself, it was watching her hit my older brother and feeling so helpless to do anything about it. That still hurts me, even today, so many years later. I looked for this woman until I was sixteen or seventeen years old, hoping that I would find her. I don't know what I would have done if I had found her, but I was very angry.

One day, many years later I came across a Scottish terrier walking by itself down the street. I remember thinking maybe that's her in old age? Well, you know how the elderly shrink? Okay, I dismissed that pretty quickly when I heard the owner yelling for the dog. I don't blame my parents for what happened because it was a different world. I guess nobody expected such a mean act, especially from someone with excellent references. I also had a clearer understanding about why I was so reluctant to let any person, no matter how impeccable their references, watch my children.

11

IT'S NOT WORTH THE THRILL

JACK

*ALL WORK AND NO PLAY MAKES
JACK A DULL BOY.*

*ALL PLAY AND NO WORK MAKES
JACK A MERE TOY.*

April, 1996
New Jersey
The Thrill Of Victory

As the year progressed, so did Georgina's commitment to her job. Getting promoted was very important to her and it seemed to me that we were heading down two different roads. My friendships were growing and most of my free time was spent with others. I was trying to alleviate my loneliness and feelings of neglect by immersing myself into new relationships. I think that most of my women friends also felt neglected, but it was really never discussed; it was just understood.

I felt bad that I had leaned on Angela so heavily for help. I tried to give back whenever I could, but she only had one child and there wasn't much she needed at that time. I decided that it would be a long friendship and things would eventually even out.

A new family had moved into the neighborhood. They had a little girl named Annie who was the same age as Rebecca. I didn't know at the time how Rebecca's friendship with Annie would become so important to me. It would shorten the amount of time I would have to spend getting her adjusted to preschool, and the way things were going, any help with any difficult situation was appreciated.

I also became friendly with Jill, Annie's mother. She seemed nice enough, but I decided not to get too close too fast. I knew that there were many types of people in this neighborhood and I was at a vulnerable stage in my life. I didn't want to make any stupid mistakes. People were making mistakes all around me and I was trying to keep things straight in my own mind.

May, 1996
New Jersey
We All Start To Waiver

I felt a lot of temptation in those days. Temptation also seemed to be affecting people around me. One afternoon, I received a call from Rachel. Rachel and I had become much friendlier since she and I had first gone with our infant daughters to playgroup and we now spoke on a regular basis. A friend of hers named Debbie, whom I had briefly met, gave Rachel her diary to read. Rachel was so taken aback with what she had read that she called me and read me the section of the diary that disturbed her.

Debbie explained in the diary that she was being completely ignored by her husband. Apparently, from Debbie's point of view, he had his mind only on his work and making more and more money. This was a common complaint among many of the women that I knew. Incredibly bored and lonely, Debbie decided she wanted to remodel her house. To keep her happy and out of his hair, her husband basically gave her *carte blanche* to do whatever she wanted. She ended up hiring a top decorator and decided to redo her entire kitchen.

The decorator took care of everything; a contractor was hired and the work started. When it came to painting the kitchen, the decorator recommended a certain painter. The painter started the job. Debbie, feeling so neglected in her marriage and taking a fancy to the painter, decided to start wearing some very provocative outfits around the painter.

As the diary set forth in expressive detail, Debbie, with preconceived intentions, started seducing the painter. Of course the painter only had so much willpower, (which I'm sure wasn't much), so he decided to paint his own Mona Lisa and make Debbie his canvas. He came, he painted, he painted and he came. I think you get the picture.

After his work on the kitchen was done, he put the final touches on Debbie and left. Debbie, somewhat distraught, didn't hear from him;

the affair was over. But as they say, hope and other things spring eternal. The decorator came back to inspect the job.

She said to Debbie in disbelief, "This is the worst job I have ever seen. I can't believe he did this. He's one of the top painters I use." (I guess she wasn't privy to the extras he bestowed on Debbie). The decorator went on to say, "I'm going to call him right now and tell him to get back over here and redo this kitchen". The painter returned and repainted everything, including Debbie, several times.

Rachel was perplexed. She knew that what Debbie had done was morally wrong, but what she wanted to discuss was whether Debbie was justified in her actions. I let out a sigh. I had heard these types of stories before from Sue. It seemed to me wherever I looked, people were searching. They seemed to have a lot of trouble finding the very thing that would make them happy. I thought of my own life and at times how lonely I felt. What made me happy? How can I achieve true happiness?

I told Rachel that I thought Debbie's motives were wrong. I was always taught that even if you're lonely and tempted, morality should prevail and there were other ways to obtain happiness.

I truly believed that, but I think at the time, I was also trying to convince myself. This was a very tough time for me. It's hard to keep thinking straight, when some people around you are bending the moral line. The very act of them widening the path seemed to justify that road to me a little more. I knew I had to put those thoughts away and stay on the right track in life. I had to be strong.

12

ACTION, REACTION

HEY, DIDDLE, DIDDLE

HEY, DIDDLE, DIDDLE,
THE CAT AND THE FIDDLE,
THE COW JUMPED OVER THE MOON,
THE LITTLE DOG LAUGHED
TO SEE SUCH A SPORT,
AND THE DISH RAN AWAY WITH THE SPOON.

June, 1996
New Jersey

The Agony Of Defeat

Another school year was coming to a close and the soccer season had just ended. Gabriella wanted to try out for the town's soccer travel team. In order to make the team, a prospective player had to try out, and then the Soccer Committee would pick the best players from that particular age group. Previously, Gabriella was playing what was called "recreation soccer." Basically, that was a league in which any person from the town who signed up for soccer had the opportunity to play.

Rachel's daughter also wanted to try out for the same travel team. I had been her daughter's coach during recreation soccer and so Rachel asked me whether I thought her daughter should try out. Rachel was of the mind that one should not go for something unless it was achievable. I suggested that her daughter go for it, because as an adult I had learned that the only time you failed at something was when you didn't try. She decided to let her daughter try out for the team.

Gabriella, after a vigorous try out, made the travel team. Rachel's daughter did not make it. Rachel took it hard, (much harder than her daughter), and she didn't talk to me for the whole summer. This was another time that I gave someone my advice and regretted that I had opened my mouth in the first place.

A little bird, another one of my friends who talked to Rachel, told me that the reason Rachel wouldn't talk to me was because I **reminded her of soccer**. Reminded her of soccer! My first thought was which part of soccer did I remind her of? Do I look exotically European? I conjured up an image of a tall, dark, thin man, impeccably dressed in an Armani designer suit with a long leather coat and very expensive Italian boots. I suddenly felt quite debonair.

The bubble burst when I remembered that she wasn't talking to me. That was not the action of someone who held you in such high regard. Then I thought: *"Perhaps she thinks I'm Euro trash and doesn't want to associate with me. Boy, these high brow people in the suburbs, there is no pleasing them."* To tell you the truth, it was hard to figure out how a great mind like Rachel's was thinking. We finally talked it over at the end of the summer and straightened everything out.

It was becoming harder and harder to figure out how women thought. I didn't understand why Rachel was so distraught about her daughter not making the team, until I remembered the messages that I received as a child. Now I knew why it affected every part of her being. For Rachel, the fact that her daughter tried wasn't enough; she had to win. She had to succeed. Rachel felt that if her daughter couldn't succeed in what she was aspiring to, then it wasn't worth her effort. That incident with Rachel gave me greater insight into my own problems.

Being Mr. Mom wasn't considered a road to success in many people's eyes. Was that the reason for my own feeling of failure? My father was now seeing me as a success so why couldn't I see myself in that same light? I knew the answer; I was the only one who would truly measure success and failure in my life. It didn't matter what anyone else thought. I wondered at that time whether I would ever really come to feel that I was a success.

The next time I talked to Rachel, I told her that I thought that winning and losing should not be perceived as absolutes, but should be based on the perspective of the person who was attempting the task. I urged her to see things differently. Her daughter won because she tried. Trying was her personal success. Rachel understood what I said and felt better about the whole situation. It all worked out pretty well. Now that I had convinced Rachel to think on a different path, there was only one thing left. All I had to do was believe it myself.

13

SPIRITUALITY

TWINKLE, TWINKLE

TWINKLE, TWINKLE, LITTLE STAR,
HOW I WONDER WHAT YOU ARE!
UP ABOVE THE WORLD SO HIGH,
LIKE A DIAMOND IN THE SKY.
TWINKLE, TWINKLE, LITTLE STAR,
HOW I WONDER WHAT YOU ARE!

September, 1996
New Jersey
Life Gets Busier

The summer seemed to fly by. I actually liked the summers and looked forward to them. Even though the kids were home and it did get a little trying at times, there wasn't the routine of school and schedules. No homework to check, no soccer, no gym class and only a few birthday parties to attend. It was a freer time for me. I could sleep in sometimes and some days just do nothing.

Jill and I were becoming closer friends and we decided that since her daughter Annie and my Rebecca were such good friends, in January we would try enrolling them in a local preschool. My thinking was that if Rebecca had a good friend with her, it would make the transition into preschool easier than it had been for Gabriella and Daniel.

In the meantime, it was approaching September and the Jewish holidays would soon begin. This was a good time to reflect upon the meaning of life and the thoughts that I was having: Why I was depressed at times and why I had such feelings of inadequacy. I decided it was time to become a more spiritual person.

I started to think about what it meant to be spiritual. I wondered: is it a learned skill, or does it take an innate ability?

That September, it became very important for me to understand how to be spiritual. I wanted to be able to teach it to my children. I concluded that spirituality went part and parcel with one of the most important lessons I could teach them: to have wisdom. They needed to be taught the wisdom to understand this complex world, and the wisdom to distinguish between the many gray areas that they would come up against in their lives.

I refused to wait until I grew old to gain the kind of wisdom that it would take to be truly insightful. I was on a quest to be wise at a fairly young age and to continue learning throughout my life.

I wanted to learn to be more of a spiritual person. I started reading some of the self-help books that took long-winded (made-up?) ways of telling me how to get in touch with my spirituality.

In one book I read that if you concentrate on the shakra it will move you to a place of Zen so you may then experience the peace and tranquility of the Millennium. Don't try this though if Mercury is in retrograde because then you may have a run in with the extra-terrestrial forces that might prove to be detrimental to your cosmic connection. Can you please tell me, **WHAT THE HELL ARE THEY TALKING ABOUT?**

I did find some real wisdom, but not in a book. It arose from a situation that presented itself on the Day of Atonement, the holiday of Yom Kippur.

October, 1996
New Jersey
An Important Lesson

Yom Kippur is the day on which Jewish people fast for twenty-five hours to ask God for forgiveness for their sins during the past year. It is one of the most important holidays in the Jewish religion.

I really look at this observance as a day of reflection, and a day to look inside yourself and see whether the path you are on, is the one on which you want to continue; regarding work, family, friends, even strangers. This is the time to really think about every facet of your life.

We went to our Temple as we do every year. I had my tickets in hand with my assigned seats posted on them. I pay for them in advance and the synagogue sends me tickets with numbers on them to show me which seats are mine, so there is no confusion.

It is an orthodox temple, so the men and the women sit separately. I walked into the synagogue with Daniel and there were two young men, perhaps in their early twenties, sitting in our seats.

I must have looked a little perplexed because the next thing I knew, an usher came up to me and asked me whether there was anything wrong. I told him that two men were sitting in our seats. There was a pause for a minute. He then asked me whether I wouldn't mind standing. He said he didn't want me to disturb the two gentlemen.

I thought about it. At the time it didn't seem like a normal request. Why would I give up my seats for people I didn't know and be forced to stand with my five-year-old? Before I answered too quickly, I thought for a minute. Maybe there was a reason for the usher's request. I decided to give him the benefit of the doubt and agreed to stand.

I stood with Daniel for thirty minutes. The two men finally got up and left the Temple. Being curious, I followed the men outside. I found one of those men crying on the shoulder of an older woman.

I learned that he and his brother were from another town and had lost their grandfather the year before. They had come back to that Temple on that day solely because their grandfather went to pray there in his final days. They were apparently very close with him and took his death extremely hard.

At that moment, I felt honored that I had relinquished my seats to the two brothers. It was so gratifying to me that I could be a part of allowing them to connect with the last place that their beloved relative had felt his spiritual bonds. I also found out that the usher had no idea why they were there. He just wanted to let them pray in peace since they were so deep in thought.

I made the right choice that day and gained a very important piece of wisdom. I obtained great insight from that usher. The usher intuitively knew what the young men needed because he was connected to the world around him. What that experience affirmed to me, was that if you **feel** a connection to the world around you, it would not send you astray.

I concluded from that experience that every child has the gift of wisdom. It's just up to the parents to bring it out. I was determined to find the way to bring Gabriella, Daniel and Rebecca in touch with their own spirit while it is still pure and still has its connection to the world. As a parent, I would not teach them to be insular, like so many people are today.

I wasn't going to confuse connecting with the issue of safety. I realized that they were two separate and distinct concepts. I was a firm believer in the "don't talk to strangers" lesson. I taught my children to be cautious. But I had a thought that if I could somehow teach Gabriella, Daniel and Rebecca to feel and be connected to the world around them, then even when they would find themselves alone they might feel less lonely.

I asked myself a question. What did God give us here on this earth that could be the very tool to develop our spirituality? That day in Temple I found the answer right in front of me: each other. Together we are mighty, alone we will fall. I realized on that day that the answers to all the mysteries in the world are found in the relationships with your spouse, your children, your family, your co-workers, your friends, your neighbors, and your community.

October, 1996
New Jersey
We Find A Sitter

I was feeling good after the holidays. I told Georgina that since she was working so hard, we should take some time and go to a movie or out to dinner alone. She reminded me about my insecurities when it came to babysitters. The thought of leaving the children with someone made me cringe. I wanted to, but the issue of safety was a real concern. As a result of my horrible experience with the Scottish babysitter, leaving my kids in the care of a stranger caused me tremendous anxiety.

I realized I would have to eventually trust someone, so I said to Georgina, "How about Nathan?" He was a sixteen-year-old boy in the neighborhood who helped me out with many projects around the house.

He babysat for Lydia and she highly recommended him. He would actually stay around for a little while after we finished a project, and play soccer with Gabriella and Daniel. They seemed to really like him.

I was nervous, but I decided to give him a try. Gabriella and Daniel were ecstatic that Nathan would be their babysitter. I told Georgina that the first time we went out we would have to make it short. She agreed and we planned our evening.

Nathan babysat that Saturday night and everything went better than expected. Gabriella, Daniel and Rebecca absolutely loved him. I felt a little threatened, but I was happy that they were so delighted. Perhaps triggered by those positive feelings that night, I revisited a time in my life when I also had very fond feeling for a babysitter.

December, 1965
Toronto, Canada
Please Play It Again

Her name was Linda and my brother, sisters and I were all very fond of her. Starting when I was seven, for two years of my life, she would baby-sit most Saturday nights. Linda had an uncanny ability to play piano by ear. At the time, being able to play like that was absolutely incredible to me. Every week, I listened to Linda and begged her to play more. Linda's playing stayed with me for years, but I never tried to play the piano myself until many years later.

At sixteen, I sat down at the keyboard and remembered how Linda played and somehow, I started to play. Maybe it was always in me, but I know that her influence was part of the reason that I went into the music business. So Linda had a hand in shaping my career choice and my many years of poverty, (thank heaven for my children's sake Nathan didn't play piano). The instability of my career, however, allowed me to become Mr. Mom and as time went on, I was really growing to love that profession.

June, 1997
New Jersey
Time Flies

The school year seemed to go by in a blur. I couldn't believe summer had come around so quickly. The plan that I had made with Jill, to put Rebecca and her daughter Annie in preschool together, was very successful. They started school in January and Rebecca's transition went very smoothly. She absolutely loved her new school and teacher. The following year Rebecca would start the same school as Gabriella and Daniel and she would go with Annie to pre-K for a full day.

Life was changing for me. Very soon I would have more time on my hands, but it didn't look like Georgina would be joining me much. She had become a true workaholic. She didn't have much time for anything but the job. That summer, since Rebecca was older, I decided I would plan many day trips with the kids. I would really give them a great summer. Angela didn't send her son to camp that summer, so together we made a list and set out to have a fun time.

It was an exhausting summer, but we had a lot of fun. At the end of that summer, I took a very hard look at myself. I saw a man who was twenty-five pounds overweight, had low self-esteem, and felt personally unsatisfied. I knew I had to do something, I just didn't know what.

September, 1997
New Jersey
Changes all around

On the first day of the new school year, with all my three children out for the day, I called Angela and asked her to meet me for lunch. We met at a small local diner. After ordering our food, for the first time in my life, I started to pour my heart out to a friend. With tears in my eyes, I started speaking about my feelings of vulnerability: "I am weak, empty, and I don't know how much longer I can go on like this. I feel lower then an amoeba. I hate who I have become."

She looked at me in disbelief. I thought she was going to leave the restaurant right then and there, but she didn't. She sat there and thought for a minute. "The gym," she said. "You and I, we need to join the gym."

I was, to say the least, a little perplexed. I had just poured my heart out to this woman and her response was "the gym." I said to her with an aggravated tone, "How is the gym supposed to help me? I have **real** problems." She looked at me and smiled and said, "It will, you just wait and see."

After I left the restaurant, I thought about Angela's suggestion. I figured that, like chicken soup, it may not help me, but it couldn't hurt. My father had been an avid runner for years. After two angioplasties, the doctors said that running saved him from having a full-blown heart attack. He used to tell me that the gym was his sanctuary. My mother always had a problem with that, but since Georgina wasn't around much, I didn't think she would have the same concerns.

I thought of another big reason that the gym might be good for me. Gabriella, Daniel and Rebecca were very strong motivations to keep myself healthy. Even one hundred and fifty years of life wouldn't be long enough to spend with them.

I started to think about all the things with which God had blessed me, and all the wonderful reasons to live. Before my lunch with Angela, I had felt very low. It amazed me how quickly I had become more optimistic about my life. The gym had already started to be a positive influence for me.

14

TWO SETS OF TEN

WHAT ARE LITTLE GIRLS MADE OF?

WHAT ARE LITTLE GIRLS MADE OF, MADE OF?
WHAT ARE LITTLE GIRLS MADE OF?
"SUGAR AND SPICE AND ALL THAT'S NICE;
AND THAT'S WHAT LITTLE GIRLS ARE
MADE OF, MADE OF."

October, 1997
New Jersey
The New Me

Angela and I joined the local gym in October of 1997. It was at that time that we decided to have a buddy system and force each other to maintain a workout program.

We got ourselves on a strict schedule. We only had so much time in the day and we needed to leave time for everything else that our households required. It helped to have a partner to work out with, because we could "guilt" each other into going, even if one of us wasn't in the mood.

Angela and I had a ritual. We would go to the gym three days a week and after we were finished at the gym we would have a quick bite so we could talk a little. I started to feel better about things quickly. The gym became a very positive outlet. The act of running also did something for me. It seemed to calm me down and it gave me a sense of accomplishment. I had more patience, which helped me with the kids.

January, 1998
New Jersey
Full Speed Ahead

About four months had passed since I joined the gym and fifteen pounds had flown off my body. I physically felt better and was starting to look more svelte. I saw Jill and she commented on how I looked like a new man. She asked me what I did to achieve my new persona. After telling her about the rewarding experience I had at the gym, she joined the same facility. I invited Jill to join Angela and me when she could.

As time went on though, Jill would ask me to go to the gym with her instead of Angela. There were times that it was more advantageous for me to go at the times that Jill suggested. Angela's other obligations would sometimes get in the way, but even on the days it wasn't convenient, I continued to go exclusively with Angela. I had given her my commitment to be partners.

It took me a long time to get Jill to understand that. She mistakenly thought I was rejecting her. Rather, I was a man of my word, and refused to go back on my promise to Angela. I am a firm believer that a person's word should be his or her bond. Georgina has always said that even a written contract is only as good as the parties behind the agreement.

The gym became more than just a place to work out. It was an ongoing social event; gossip reigned supreme. I found the social aspects of the gym therapeutic. It became part of my work out. I always tried to leave time to talk. I was amazed at what people told each other. I was privy to all kinds of information. Aside from the gossip, it became very apparent that most of the women were there to make their bodies as lean and mean as humanly possible. That quest didn't stop there.

If some of these women couldn't achieve that objective through exercise, then all kinds of surgery was not out of the question. I'm not exaggerating; I would need a filing cabinet to categorize all the different types of body add-ons and adjustments that these various women told me about. Maybe I'm dating myself, but if you remember the show *The Bionic Woman*, I can tell you for a fact, she has arrived, and with more than just a fake arm and leg.

March, 1997
New Jersey
Work Out, At All Costs

Angela called me up one morning and asked me whether I could go to the gym earlier than usual. The kids were off from school for Spring break. I had never used the babysitting services at the gym, but I thought that the way the room was set up, I could have my eyes on them constantly. There was an over-sized glass window on the wall of the babysitting room, which provided a clear view of the children. I asked Gabriella whether she would watch Daniel, Rebecca and Angela's son in the gym's babysitting facility while Angela and I had a quick workout. I could see the children from where I was exercising so I thought there would be no problems during my forty-minute program.

The supervision, in my opinion, was not up to the standard to which I had become accustomed with Nathan. The children were not abused or mistreated in any way. They were, to put it bluntly, ignored. It looked to me like the children were treated like cute little hamsters that were placed in a secure glass aquarium, so they would not cause any annoyance to the gym, their mothers, (or in my case fathers), the other patrons or their caretakers.

I had my eyes on the kids the entire time I was there, but when I noticed two other children it ended up giving me a depressing workout. A set of twins had their faces pressed up against the glass of the baby-sitting room, with tears streaking down their cheeks. They looked so painfully pathetic. Their mother was paged three times out of her spin class, a place in the gym where a group of people assemble in a big room, sit down on stationary bicycles and ride vigorously to get nowhere for about one hour.

The last time she was paged she was so irate that I could hear her instructing the babysitters that if they called her again, she would not respond. I thought the woman must have been dizzy from spinning. I couldn't understand how she could have such a compulsive need to return to her inane exercise class, at the cost of ignoring her two children.

After this went on for a little while, I went over to the babysitting room and asked Gabriella to include the twins in the game that she was playing with the other kids. It seemed to make things better, but we had to leave before the twins did and the look on their faces really pulled on my heartstrings.

April, 1997
New Jersey
Like Father, Like Son

I was feeling stronger and stronger. I had become a runner, like my father. I guess the apple really doesn't fall far from the tree after all. Another advantage of running was that I had something in common with my father, which made my relationship with him even more rewarding.

The weather was getting better and so I decided to try to run outside instead of on the treadmill. That was a big mistake. There was a fallen branch on the sidewalk that I had to jump over and I landed in an awkward way. I pulled a muscle in my upper thigh, which put me out of commission for a while. My dad told me to make sure I stretched for at least a week before I attempted to run again.

Angela told me about a good trainer at the gym that could help me with stretching. I decided to try one session. It was very expensive, so I was hoping that one training exercise would be enough, and then I could continue to rehabilitate on my own.

The trainer was a woman. She was in her early thirties and her name was Lila. She was slim and very attractive and I noticed that she was wearing a thong body suit over a leotard. It was one of those outfits that was held together by a string in the back that went right into the crack of her ass. I had seen women wear this kind of attire before, but didn't understand why. It had to be uncomfortable. As far as I was concerned, it was like getting a constant wedgie. I remember getting wedgies when I was younger and it was no fun. Why would you want to buy an outfit that gave you a perpetual one?

Lila started stretching me out on the floor mats. After a while, we went over to the step machines. She told me that until I was fully recovered, it would be better to use a stepper instead of running. She demonstrated how the machine worked. I was watching her from behind, and with every step she took the thread which held her outfit together, was hiking further and further north. If that piece of string had gone any higher, she could have used it to floss her teeth. I was so fixated on her outfit that I didn't focus on what she was telling me.

I totally wasted that whole part of the training session. I had no idea how to use that stupid machine and at that point I didn't care. All that filled my mind was how Lila would need to use a pair of tweezers to get that piece of material out of her buttocks. When she got off the machine I thanked Lila for the session, and decided to just take it easy until I felt better.

The gym crowd was a very diverse group. Some of the people I liked and some I didn't. It seemed to me to be a microcosm of the larger world. I think, though, that the one thing we all had in common was that no matter who we were, the very act of working out was a step in the right direction. At least for me, it was a good turn in my life.

15

THE PURSUIT OF HAPPINESS

HIGH DIDDLE

HIGH DIDDLE DOUBT, MY CANDLE'S OUT
MY WIFE IS NOT AT HOME;
SADDLE MY HOG AND BRIDLE MY DOG,
AND FETCH MY WIFE TO ME HOME.

June, 1997
New Jersey
Till Death Do We Part?

Everything was going well. It was approaching the end of another successful school year for the kids and my personal growth was moving along in the right direction. I only had one complaint, but unfortunately it was a big one. Georgina and I were continuing to move down separate roads. I had good friends, my children were wonderful, but when the dust cleared, would I have a wife?

I tried to talk to her about the lack of attention she was giving me, but my words fell on deaf ears. I was very hurt about the situation and as a defense I started to close myself off.

One night we had a big fight. I don't even remember what it was about. All I recall is leaving the house and taking a walk around our neighborhood. I thought about the Declaration of Independence. That certain truths were "self-evident"; that we are endowed by our Creator with certain unalienable rights, among them is the pursuit of happiness. I thought, *"Why couldn't our forefathers have written into the Declaration **how** we could obtain that happiness?"* I guess if they knew the answer to that question, they wouldn't have been human. It became apparent to me that there was no easy answer; no magic pill. There was only an ongoing search to find my own individual happiness.

In late June, Georgina started to feel a little sick. We thought it was a flu and that it would run its course. After a week of being ill and consulting the doctor for the second time, we were told that she had a very stubborn virus and she should take a couple of weeks off from work and stay home.

My birthday was coming up on July fourth and Georgina surprised me with four corporate seats for the band "Chicago", who were playing at the PNC Art Center. I was to choose another couple to go with us.

Since Georgina didn't feel that well, she suggested that instead of inviting another couple, I should ask three of my women friends. I didn't feel right about going without her, but she insisted.

July, 1997
New Jersey
Through Music, Comes Introspection

After Georgina gave me the tickets, I realized that asking some of my women friends to this event would become a little more involved than just a couple of friends going to a concert. I wasn't sure how their husbands would react.

I asked Angela first and she responded positively right away. Her husband has a very open mind, and trusts her implicitly. Lydia and Rachel turned me down. They didn't tell me that their husbands didn't want them to go, but I knew that this was the case. Jill said that she would go no matter what her husband said.

I had one more ticket and no one to use it. Angela and Jill told me that their husbands wanted to go, but I had two reasons not to ask them. One, I didn't want to choose one over the other. I didn't think that was fair. Two, neither Jill nor Angela wanted their husbands there. They were excited about going alone with just friends. So I had to find another open-minded fool, I mean husband, who would allow his wife to go.

I tried one more woman that I knew. Her name was Julie. I didn't hang out with her that much so I didn't hold out much hope. To my surprise, the long shot came in and she said yes.

The night finally arrived, and we agreed as a group to go for dinner before the concert. I decided to drive all of us; I thought it would make things easier with the parking situation. Jill picked a little place in a nearby town to have dinner. It was a cute little Italian restaurant. I really wasn't in the mood for Italian food, but lacking a better alternative, I decided to go along with it.

When we arrived at the restaurant, we were all in one of those rambunctious playful moods. The restaurant wasn't very crowded so we were seated immediately. As soon as the waiter came to the table, I started in on Jill. Most of the time Jill acts like she's not all with it; kind of an airhead. I personally think it's just an act. I think she uses it to her advantage. But regardless of the act, I took the liberty of setting up a joke between her and the waiter.

After telling the waiter that we were going to the concert, we arranged for a rendezvous between Jill and him at the end of his shift that night. She was supposed to bring back the leftovers to the restaurant and she and the waiter were to indulge in a late supper. What a date! Leftovers until sunrise; it sounded almost too good to eat. Jill had a good sense of humor, even when it was at her own expense. I think we really had the waiter going because he tried to slip Jill his phone number before we left the restaurant.

After dinner we proceeded to the Chicago concert. The seats we had were wonderful. We were sitting in a section that was cordoned off just for the corporate sponsors of the event. There was also a corporate hospitality tent that our tickets admitted us into. I felt like an elitist fat cat. I have to tell you it wasn't a bad feeling. I now had a small glimpse into how the bigwigs lived and it wasn't too shabby. It was a nice birthday present.

There were only four seats in the row. I had to make the decision of who sat where. I decided to put Angela beside me, Julie beside her, and Jill on the end. I don't think Jill liked that very much. She was kept out of some of the conversation because of her positioning, but it was the way it seemed to work out the best at the time.

Directly in front of Angela, there was an elderly man who started moving his behind around on his seat. At first I thought he was practicing some ritual prayer. "Please God, allow these has-beens to be at least half as good as they once were." It seemed like a reasonable prayer at the time. After a couple of minutes Julie turned to Angela and said something about the man. I didn't quite hear what she said, but it soon became evident.

I felt like I was in an episode of the sitcom *Seinfeld*; the one where Kramer fed chili to the horse Rusty and Rusty proceeded to pass gas until the people in the carriage couldn't breathe anymore. The elderly man was Rusty in human form. He was relentless. He would move around and POW, another wave hit us. It finally ended about half an hour into the concert when this gentleman, (and I use the term loosely), left his seat for about 15 minutes.

When he returned we were all nervous, but the air remained clear. Thank God he was willing to miss some of the concert to expel what had died inside him that night. I have to tell you it gave a new meaning to the words corporate pig. As horrific as the smell was it certainly made for a fun evening and even better storytelling later.

After the concert, I drove the women home. I decided to drop them in this order. First, Julie, then Angela and lastly Jill (since she lived the closest to my house). But after I dropped off Angela something happened that I never expected.

Almost as soon as Jill and I left Angela's house, Jill turned to me and said, "Is something going on between you and Angela?" I must admit that I was very taken aback by the question.

I quickly answered her with a decisive "No." Jill went on, "People have been talking about the fact that you guys go to the gym together and have been seen having lunch many times alone." I told Jill that even if I would entertain such an idea, which I certainly did not, I would have too much to lose for giving into a very base instinct.

First and most importantly, I would lose my wife and my family, both of whom I loved dearly. Secondly, I would eventually have to give up my friendship with Angela because I don't believe that people can stay friends after an extra-marital affair—too much baggage. I told Jill that I had worked too hard on both my family and my friendship to foolishly sacrifice either or both.

I then became depressed. I could see that I had naively and stupidly believed that you could achieve closeness with someone without it being perceived as something sordid. It now became clear to me that once that closeness involved a man and a woman as friends, people automatically assumed it was an affair.

After I dropped Jill off and came home, I thought about what was said to me that night and I had two concerns. One, what if rumors should come back to my children. It might hurt them. I knew I would have to educate them and explain to my kids that this is my job. It entails my being friendly with women and there is nothing wrong with that. Two, I wondered what Georgina thought. Like an idiot, I had never considered what she might have been feeling.

I went upstairs and Georgina was half-asleep. I woke her and asked her whether she trusted me. She mumbled, "What?" She started to wake up and I asked again, "Do you trust me with my women friends?" she said, "Yes, absolutely." I asked her, "Why?" She replied, "I remember how we started, when we met, and the foundation that our marriage is built on. Maybe I am stupid and naive, but I choose to believe in us. Now go to sleep." Those words, "believe in us," rang in my ears half the night. I started to think back to the time we met.

April, 1983
New York City
A Match Made In Heaven

It was a whirlwind romance. I was living in Los Angeles at the time. My parents lived in Canada and, as a Holocaust survivor, my father was asked to come to the Holocaust convention in Washington, DC. There was a ground breaking ceremony and dedication on the site of what is now the U.S. Holocaust Museum. Even though it was last minute, when my father arrived in Washington on a Sunday afternoon, he decided to call me and asked whether I would join him at the convention. He told me that if I didn't arrive by the next morning to forget it because the convention lasted only three days.

Although I would have preferred to have more notice, I decided that it might be a rewarding experience to go to the convention. I hung up the phone and started to call the airlines to see whether I could get a ticket. All the airlines were completely booked from Los Angeles to Washington. The only available ticket was first-class. It was about four thousand dollars round trip. Rockefeller I wasn't, so I called my father back and told him that I was very sorry, but on such short notice, I could not get a reasonably priced airline ticket.

That seemed to be the end of that, case closed. Although I was disappointed, I accepted that fate had dealt its cards, but around 5:00 that evening, on a whim, I decided to tempt that fate and I called Delta Airlines. I had called them before, but I had a feeling that things had changed for some reason. I asked them one more time whether they had any economy tickets to Washington.

The reservation agent for Delta said to me "Mr. Wertman we just had a cancellation. I can get you on a plane at 8:00 p.m. at a price of two hundred and fifty dollars, which is the lowest price in the market." I quickly said, "I'll take it." The agent then gave me a reservation number and told me to give that number to the person at the Delta counter at the airport.

After I arrived at the airport, I proceeded to the counter and gave my reservation number to the ticketing agent. I found out that there were no two hundred and fifty-dollar tickets on that flight. The only seats that were left were in first class. I explained that I had been given an economy reservation and needed to leave for Washington that night. The ticketing agent told me to wait for a moment while she checked with a supervisor.

Another woman walked over to the computer screen. After reviewing the screen she said, "Mr. Wertman, this is very unusual, but you seem to be holding a first class ticket for two hundred and fifty dollars. I don't understand it, but enjoy your flight." I was on the plane that night flying first class to Washington DC.

The convention was emotionally moving to say the least. Listening to the survivors' relive their experiences of such a horrifying event was something I'll never forget.

I decided that since I was already on the East Coast, I would go up to New York City for business. I had some contacts with a few record companies and I wanted to play them my new songs.

While I was in Washington, I had mentioned to my father that I was going to New York after the convention. One of my father's closest friends was also going to New York. He was taking a hotel room that he offered to share with me. This wouldn't cost me anything, so I decided I couldn't pass up the opportunity to go to New York relatively inexpensively.

My father's friend told me to call him the day I was leaving and we would hook up and go together. This trip was turning out to be great. I had flown first class to Washington and now it wasn't going to cost me anything to stay in New York. On the day I was leaving though, a strange thing happened. When I called my father's friend's room, he had already checked out and no one knew where he was. He also hadn't told me in which hotel in New York he was staying, so I couldn't look him up in the city. This wasn't like him; he was a very responsible person.

After trying to track him down, I decided I had better leave or I would miss my plane. I had my father drive me to the Washington airport and since I didn't know where I would be in New York, I didn't leave my father any forwarding address or phone number.

Before the opportunity to stay with my father's friend had come up, my friend Pete from Los Angeles had given me the phone number of a woman (a family friend of his) in New York City. He had told me to call her and she might be able to help me find a hotel that was not too expensive for the two nights I planned to be in New York.

When I arrived in New York, I immediately called the woman to whom Pete had referred me. I asked her whether she knew of any reasonably priced hotels in New York. She told me that there weren't any reasonably priced hotels in New York City. She said that since she trusted Pete and she had a spare couch, if I wanted to I could stay one night at her place. We agreed to meet at her apartment building; she said I would be able to recognize her because she was wearing a tan trench coat over a purple suit. I sat in the lobby waiting for her. I remember wondering what she would look like. She finally arrived.

She came striding in, moving about ten times faster than the average human being. I, having come from the convention in Washington, felt very mellow and was moving very slowly. She walked straight through the lobby, expecting me to follow her. I had to run to catch up. Abruptly, she stopped, turned around, looked straight into my eyes and smiled. I looked directly back at her and something happened. It was like time itself stopped. I had a strange feeling that I was part of another world. I could see right through her, right down into her very soul. With an incredible feeling of warmth, I knew I had found my other half. I was about to become whole. I felt complete.

She took me up to her apartment, gave me a set of keys and showed me about four times how to work the five different locks on her door. I was living in Los Angeles at the time and I was no stranger to crime, but five locks on the door was a little much even for me. She said, "I'm Georgina; Welcome to New York" and then she hurried back to her high-pressured Park Avenue law job.

When I went into Georgina's apartment, I felt like I had come home. It was so comfortable. I waited about an hour and then called her at the office. I wanted to thank her, so I asked whether I could buy her dinner as a gesture of gratitude for letting me stay the night. Okay, so it was an excuse to spend some social time with her, but it worked like a charm.

Even though she made a point of telling me that she always worked through dinner and ate at her desk, she was making an exception for me because I knew no one in New York, and she appreciated my thoughtfulness. We ended up going out to a great deli and talking for the next two days straight. I realize I was only supposed to stay one night, but what can I say, there are no limits when dealing with *amore*.

When I left on that Saturday, for the entire flight from New York to Los Angeles, I couldn't get Georgina out of my mind. I replayed many of our conversations. I loved her warmth and energy. Her thoughts about children, religion, political beliefs and family values really interested me. We had so much in common. It was amazing. As soon as I landed, I went to the first pay phone and called her from LAX airport. I told her that we would be married. She replied "You are absolutely crazy." But I was in love with her, and I knew that we belonged together.

After my return to Los Angeles, we talked on the phone every day and every night. After two weeks she came to visit me. I remember it like it was yesterday—the anticipation of waiting at the airport for the flight to arrive. I was like a nervous little boy hoping that the magic that had started in New York would continue.

It did continue and two weeks after that I went back to New York to visit her. On that trip to New York I asked her to come up to Toronto to meet my parents. We went there separately; she had to finish a project with a Toronto-based company that she was already working on when we met.

When I arrived in Canada I told my parents I wanted to marry the girl that they were going to meet that night. I guess I kind of dropped a bomb on them. My father sat me down and asked me one question. "Are you really sure that you want to do this after knowing her for such a short time?" I told him I was never so sure of anything in my life and that I was ready to create the beauty in a marriage just like my mother and he had done. It was a cheesy line but I think it drove the point home.

After Georgina met my parents, we returned to New York and I was getting ready to pop the question. I wanted to think of a creative way to do it. So one night, which was a month after we met, Georgina came home to her apartment and I had made her dinner. It was honey-garlic chicken. I pride myself on being a pretty good cook.

After the meal, she said to me, "Any guy that can cook like that, I should marry." I knew she wasn't serious with her comment on marriage, but that was exactly what I had in mind at the moment. Nervously, I then took out a box wrapped with beautiful ribbon and gave it to her. Georgina opened it. There was a tee-shirt inside. The front of the shirt had the words: "Georgina I love you. Will you marry me?" She broke down and started crying. There was a pause, only for a couple of seconds, but the longest I can remember in any situation in my life. Georgina then looked at me with her teary eyes and replied "Yes." I then gave her the engagement ring to make it official.

We were married five months later. We were impulsive, impetuous, foolhardy, and too romantic, but very much in love. I believed that fortune had brought me to that Holocaust convention and providence had guided me to Georgina. I saw the start of my own family arise out of the ashes and remembrance of my father's family.

My thoughts drifted back to the present time. Georgina was my gift. I had to treat her with care. I could make this gift in my life something of beauty, or I could destroy it until it became like a discarded, withered plant. I decided that night, to nourish my marriage again and try to go forward.

August, 1997
New Jersey
The Virus Gets Worse

My decision to work on my marriage was not going to bear any fruit if it was only me who chose to do so. I had to somehow get Georgina to stop and listen to what I was saying. Unfortunately, that wasn't happening. She was still very consumed with work, until a small tick changed everything.

The virus that she had earlier in the summer had never resolved itself. Joint pains now accompanied her flu-like symptoms. The doctors conducted all kinds of tests but found nothing concrete.

We had a family vacation scheduled in late August to Colonial Williamsburg, Virginia. We drove there expecting to stay for a week, but the trip didn't last more than two days. In Williamsburg Georgina became very ill with a fever and body pains, and I found myself driving a hundred miles an hour back to New Jersey, straight to Robert Wood Johnson University Hospital. After hours in the emergency room, and a battery of diagnostic tests, she was finally diagnosed with Lyme disease.

We were told that Georgina had contracted the disease, which was carried by infectious deer ticks, sometime at the beginning of the summer. In her case, because of the late diagnosis, she would have complications. Although she was treated with antibiotics that rid her of the Lyme disease after a few months, the Lyme had triggered Rheumatoid Arthritis, a long-term degenerative disease of the joints that, while mostly manageable, had no cure.

I had wanted her to slow down, but not at this cost. She was at home for the next month, regaining her strength and going to physical therapy. Even after that the doctors advised her to take it easy. Georgina informed her boss that she would be able to work full-time, but had to telecommute one day of every week to give her body a rest from the long drive. It turned out that she received a rude awakening when her boss wasn't as understanding as she had hoped he would have been.

October, 1997
New Jersey
You're Only As Good As Your Last Hit

Her immediate boss said to her, "Putting your health aside, do you think that telecommuting is good for the department? What kind of message does it send to the other people?" *Putting your health aside?* Was this guy from the same planet as us? Is there anything more important than your health? I was amazed when Georgina told me this. She became very distraught. She couldn't believe the lack of support that she had received. She had worked extremely hard for the company for many years and was asking for an accommodation that she felt was reasonable. After some negotiation involving more senior people in the company, it was agreed that Georgina could work from home one day a week. The battle had left her somewhat disenchanted about her fierce loyalty to her job and what she was getting in return.

I think that was the time that Georgina started to take stock of her life. Call it a wake-up call, call it a moment of clarity, call it whatever you like. I know that there are middle-aged men who have heart attacks and go through the same kind of self-analysis or mid-life examination. Whatever it was, I know that Georgina started to reflect upon what was truly important to her and what she ultimately wanted to achieve in life. She talked to me at length about our relationship; we discussed our feelings and communicated on a level that we had not achieved in quite some time. I felt that we were still on different paths that were divergent from our common road, but at least now we were **both** walking towards a point where our paths could again become one.

16

THE INFORMATION AGE

THERE WAS A CROOKED MAN

THERE WAS A CROOKED MAN,
AND HE WALKED A CROOKED MILE.
HE FOUND A CROOKED STILE;
HE BOUGHT A CROOKED CAT,
WHICH CAUGHT A CROOKED MOUSE,
AND THEY ALL LIVED TOGETHER
IN A LITTLE CROOKED HOUSE.

October, 1997
New Jersey
Too Much, Too Soon

October of 1997 brought a very different school experience. Daniel's first grade class was greatly tuned in to many things that I thought I would not have to deal with until some time in the future. One blustery day in the middle of October, Daniel came home asking many questions. One of his classmates, a little girl named Jenny, told Daniel that after her parents put her to sleep she heard something in their bathroom and decided to go and explore.

The bathroom door was slightly open. She looked in and, as she put it, she saw her parents "sexing it." There were candles lit all around the tub, and there was a romantic glow emanating from her father's face. Then Jenny explained to Daniel that her father got this "weird" look on his face while her mother went "scuba diving" in the bath. She then told Daniel that his friend Tommy saw the same thing on a video over at Zach's house.

Apparently, at this point they brought Tommy into the conversation. Daniel told me that Tommy was over at Zach's three days before and Zach took Tommy upstairs and brought out some of his father's favorite videos. The two boys started to watch one.

This particular video (I guess his father's moist, I mean most favorite), was a very explicit porno flick. It showed, among other things, a man and a woman having oral sex. The two first-graders found this video very entertaining and decided to share the details of the movie with some of the girls in the class.

I didn't know how to explain this to Daniel. I was about to say something when the phone rang. It was Angela. The first words out of her mouth were "Did you hear what the boys learned in school today?" I told her that I was just talking about it with Daniel. Just then I heard a beep. It was my call waiting. I told Angela to hold on for a minute and

I clicked over. Julie was on the other line. She said, "Mark, you're not going to believe what Sam just told me!"

I told Julie that I would call her right back because Angela was on the other line. While this entire phone drama was going on, my poor Daniel was standing there right in front of me waiting for answers. I told Angela, who was still hanging on, that I would call her back. I then sat down with Daniel and looked him right in the eyes and said, "Daniel, sometimes in life there are questions that come up that can't be quite answered at the time of the inquiry." (I started to put my politician hat on.) I stumbled on, "Those questions are the very things that make this situation so difficult, but we all know it is good to ask questions because many times questions are how we learn things." He didn't know what I was talking about at that point, which was the whole idea. Then the jig was up. Daniel said to me, "Daddy, I don't understand what you're saying; I'll just ask Mummy when she gets home." I must admit that worked for me.

November, 1997
Loose Lips Sink Ships

The first Sunday in November, Jenny, the little girl with the "sexing it" story was having her sixth birthday party. The entire first grade class was invited, including Daniel. Angela, Julie and I had been talking about the incident. By that time, every parent from the class knew about the event, except Jenny's parents. News with a juicy headline travels fast. After talking about it, Angela, Julie and I felt that someone should say something so Jenny's parents could talk to her.

What Jenny had told her classmates was having a big effect on the other children, so we felt that maybe her parents could explain what she had seen in a more acceptable way. Near the end of the party, Angela suggested that I go talk to Jenny's father and tell him, man-to-man, about what had transpired between his daughter and the rest of the class.

I thought about it for a minute. I concluded that since he was a man, I could tap into the Macho thing. "Hey stud, I heard you got lucky a couple of weeks ago. We should all be **that** lucky. You the man!" I would build him up for a while and then tell him that everyone knew about his triumphant victory. Then I would segue into telling him that his daughter had seen everything, and suggest that perhaps he or his wife could talk to Jenny. Maybe they could tell her that Mommy and Daddy are in love and when two people are in love and married, then what she witnessed was a normal and beautiful thing. After that he could prance around at school events like a stallion (at least until the end of the year, by which time some other drama would probably have captured everyone's imagination).

When was I going to learn? My past experience had taught me that whenever I tried to give advice, I usually had regrets. My whole little planned conversation backfired. When I told Jenny's father what had happened, he felt incredibly embarrassed. Apparently he is a very shy man. He disappeared for the rest of the party. He didn't even come out for the cake.

I felt awful and tried to find the nearest rock to crawl under. I thought I was doing him a service, but sometimes your best game plan can turn out wrong if it is not completely thought out and you don't know the players. I had bad timing and had used bad judgment. The road I had headed down when talking to Jenny's dad was paved with good intentions, but even the best-motivated strategy can go astray. I sincerely hoped Jenny's father put his embarrassment aside and that somehow things worked out for his daughter and the family.

November, 1997
New Jersey
Liar Liar Pants On Fire

I tried to put the Jenny incident out of my mind, but before I could become too complacent, Daniel came home with another problem. There was a boy named Gary, in his first grade class, who lied compulsively. On occasion, Daniel had play dates with him, but Gary's lying became so pervasive that Daniel started to ask me not to make any more arrangements for them to get together. I couldn't be sure that there was an ounce of truth that came out of this kid's mouth.

Gary would lie and say he had been certain places, owned certain toys and games, or knew certain people. I believe he was trying to make himself seem more important and get attention. Tiring of his falsehoods, one-by-one his classmates began to shun him. As you might remember, first grade can be a rough place. What I couldn't believe was that even at those times when I caught Gary in a lie, and confronted him, he had the audacity to keep lying right to my face.

I think Gary believed that if you stick to the lie you're telling, you will have no problem. I guess it worked for him because one day in November Daniel came home very upset. He told me that about half the class had been chatting when they shouldn't have. The teacher became angry and asked for a show of hands from the children who were talking.

Daniel put up his hand. Gary, who was also talking, didn't raise his hand. Daniel was punished and was told that he had to write an apology letter to the teacher for his bad behavior.

Daniel said to me, "Daddy I know I was wrong, but Gary was talking and he didn't get punished because he wasn't honest and didn't raise his hand. If I wouldn't have put up my hand but had kept quiet and lied, like Gary, then I wouldn't have had to do this stupid letter." I could hear where this was going. Daniel was seeing the virtue in lying and saw for the first time that life was not always just.

I told him that sometimes life was unfair, but telling the truth was still the best way because lying would always come back to haunt you. He listened to me and he accepted my answer and went to do his assignment.

I sat there after Daniel had left and my stomach was gripped with an old fear and I remembered the tears I had shed over a terrible wrong. I was no stranger to the repercussions and the guilt-ridden feelings that accompany a lie. I had carried the burden of a falsification around with me for many years.

May, 1975
Toronto, Canada
Schools Out

I was never a very good student. I had my strengths here and there, but overall did not perform very well in school. My skills were never at a high enough level in any given year to allow me to succeed at that particular grade's curriculum. I was always playing catch-up, and I hated being in that horrible position.

In Canada there are thirteen grades of school. The next level of education is college or university. As I entered high school, and my grades continued to decline, I eventually lost interest in school altogether. By twelfth grade, I hardly attended classes anymore. I would show up at school in the morning, sit in on homeroom and then proceed to the music center and practice piano all day. I wasn't trained as a musician but I loved to play by ear. It was an escape for me. I was a lost soul, had no direction, and felt that I had very few options.

One day when I came home, the mail had just been delivered. I didn't usually bring the mail into the house, but something told me on that day that I should. When I took the letters out of the box, I noticed that there was something from the high school. I had a sinking feeling—the one you get when you've done something terribly wrong and judgment day is just around the corner.

I decided to open it. There was a note from the school explaining to my parents that because I had failed to attend classes, I was considered to have dropped out of school. I was officially a high school dropout. I started to feel sick inside. With a lack of wisdom on my part and a lack of respect for the two people that I cared most about, I chose to destroy the note.

A couple of days later, my mother asked me how I was doing in school. I continued to live my lie and answered, "Okay." Every morning I would wake up and pretend I was going to school. I would take the same books with me in the morning and bring them home at night. The whole thing broke down about a month later, when a friend of mine happened to see my mother and asked her whether I was working. They hadn't seen me in regular school classes and had wondered what I'd been doing.

When my parents confronted me, it was one of the hardest moments in my life. How could I have lied to them? What possessed me? I was embarrassed and I was a coward. I hadn't remembered the most important lesson they had taught me. It rang clear in my mind that day: "There is **nothing** you can't tell us; there is nothing that bad." Even with those words that were spoken over and over again in our home, I was too frightened to speak the truth, but on that day, I came clean and took my punishment.

Although my parents forgave me, I didn't realize how strong the punishment for lying would be—a lifetime of never forgiving myself for what I considered such an egregious act. Now I stood there many years later with my son and wondered whether one day he would also lie to me. I had gained back my parents' respect after years of demonstrating my thoughtfulness and honesty. I thought that with that effort, I would finally be able to forgive myself. The reality is, however, that with the man in my mirror, I am and will always be, my own harshest judge.

One day, I knew I would have to undertake one of the hardest tasks a person can do in life. I would have to admit to a blunder, which caused me great embarrassment. I would sit down and tell Gabriella, Daniel and Rebecca about my lie to their grandparents, in hopes that they would avoid repeating their father's stupidity.

December, 1997
Palm Springs
Siblings

It was the beginning of December and I was looking forward to the holidays. Georgina's company shut down between Christmas and New Years Day every year, which gave all employees a nice paid vacation. We were going to Palm Springs that year to visit my parents.

They lived in a condominium for about four months out of the year to escape the cold winters in Toronto. The reason that my mother and father chose Palm Springs as their getaway was because Palm Springs was only two hours from Los Angeles by car. Since my family and I, as well as my older brother Joel, were all living in Los Angeles, staying in Palm Springs gave my parents a chance to see their two sons and some of their grandchildren.

My brother Joel, who continued to live in Los Angeles after Georgina and I moved to New Jersey, went to Palm Springs regularly to visit my parents throughout the winter. As a matter of fact, last year he purchased a condominium there to use for the winter months.

My father and my brother didn't get along that well and I knew it hurt my dad deeply. On numerous occasions I spoke to Joel, and tried to get him to talk to our father and see whether he could patch things up. Unfortunately, during this year their relationship really deteriorated.

Joel, who is in his second marriage, had been intent on creating a good relationship, (I believe at his wife's request), between our parents and his new in-laws. His wife was pregnant and she believed in one big, happy family. My parents don't enjoy being with Joel's in-laws. They had problems with them at his wedding and didn't want to become too friendly. They tried to accommodate their son sometimes, but when the relationship was pushed too frequently, they would make up excuses to get out of certain social situations.

The weekend before we arrived in Palm Springs that year, my brother Joel was there. He invited our parents to his condo, for an early brunch with his in-laws. My parents declined the invitation. At the time, they really were busy, but Joel knew they didn't want to attend.

On the day our parents refused the invitation, Joel was visiting them alone, without his wife. He was clearly very upset. Our mother decided not to play games anymore. She felt very awkward about the whole situation. With much resolve, she sat her son down and told him truthfully that there was no love lost between his in-laws and them, and he shouldn't push the relationship. Joel totally lost it and stormed out of the house.

It didn't end there. My parents didn't hear from Joel for approximately two days. As the hostility continued, my mother felt terrible. She called me and explained the incident, and said she was planning to call Joel and try to talk this problem through in a rational manner. I thought it was a good idea to talk, before the situation became worse. I offered to help. Unfortunately, before she could make that call, the situation escalated.

My parents try to take a walk together every morning. There is a bike/walking path that they use. It was a Saturday when Joel had stormed out of our parents' house. On the following Monday, my parents were taking their usual walk on the path. There was a fence separating the path and the golf course on one side and a fence separating the path and a trailer camp on the other side.

As my parents were walking, my father saw someone in the distance on a bicycle. When this person saw my father he sped up, and as he passed my mother, he didn't hit her, but did drive her into the fence on the golf course side. My mother looked at my father and said, "Who was the maniac on that bike? He almost killed me." To my mother's surprise my father told her that it was their son Joel.

The situation became disastrous. It felt like I was about to vacation in a war zone. I knew that there was no way that Joel had intentionally tried to hurt our mother. He panicked and couldn't face our parents. It was a joke among the rest of my siblings. Joel became the "unicycler," a play on words, referring to the unibomber. We would imagine Joel as Artie Johnson, the actor who played the little old man, on the 60's TV show *Laugh-In*, with his tricycle trying to hit Ruth Buzzi, the little old lady.

December, 1997
Palm Springs
Do You Have A First Aid Kit?

The whole thing was a mess. When we arrived in Palm Springs Joel and my parents were not speaking, but all I talked about with my parents was Joel, and all I talked about with Joel was my parents. I felt like I was in the middle of a stupid argument and I was expected to take sides.

As a father, I've seen my children fight, but the immaturity of this feud far surpassed anything I had ever witnessed before. I was helpless in trying to patch up anything between my parents and their firstborn son. I left Palm Springs hoping that Joel would call them and straighten things out.

March, 1998
New Jersey
I Was Still Trying

It had been over two months since I was back from Palm Springs and since that time, Joel had no contact with our parents. It was almost my mother's birthday and all of us were wondering whether Joel would make an appearance or a phone call for a birthday wish.

On her birthday, before I had a chance to call her, my mother called me, crying. She told me that unannounced, Joel came over to their house in Palm Springs, and in a very half-hearted way, had wished her a happy birthday. Because of the situation building up over the last few months, she could not hold back anymore, and let all her anger to come to the surface. It developed into another huge fight, with each of them literally pointing fingers at the other.

I tried to calm her down on the phone and told her that everything would eventually work out. Shortly after my mother's birthday, Joel's wife gave birth to a baby boy. Our parents, who were back in Canada at the time, decided to make the three thousand mile trip to see their grandson just after the birth. That effort somewhat restored relations. I was very happy. It's hard to have fights within your own family. They cause you the greatest amount of pain. The conflict between my parents and my brother was not ideal, but at least there was an effort being made, which eased the tension for the rest of us.

17

PERFECTION TO GO

GREGORY GRIGGS

GREGORY GRIGGS, GREGORY GRIGGS,
HAD TWENTY-SEVEN DIFFERENT WIGS,
HE WORE THEM UP, HE WORE THEM DOWN,
TO PLEASE THE PEOPLE OF THE TOWN.
HE WORE THEM EAST, HE WORE THEM WEST,
BUT HE NEVER COULD TELL WHICH ONE HE LIKED BEST.

April, 1998
New Jersey
A Hair Raising Experience

Every visit I had with my father brought us closer. It was an extremely rewarding experience for me, but it didn't do what I thought it would. I thought that if I achieved my father's approval and respect, it would somehow make me feel better about myself. To my disappointment, that improved relationship wasn't helping my own self worth.

Continuing to be unsatisfied inside myself, I looked towards my own outside physical appearance. By going to the gym three days a week, I was thinner and felt better about my appearance. I started to take notice of all the hair transplant commercials that were so prevalent on television. My hair was very thin on top and the thought of more hair became an enticing idea. I began talking to Georgina about the new drugs that were being touted to restore hair and asked her to research them.

Since Georgina worked at a major pharmaceutical company, I thought she would have access to the current research and development news on the subject of hair-growth medicines. Before I went too far, I mentioned to Gabriella that maybe I would try one of those new drugs on the market and asked her how she would like her daddy with a full head of hair.

She got very upset and ran off to her room. I went upstairs, knocked on her door, entered her room and asked her why she was so upset. There were tears in Gabriella's eyes as she responded to me with a question. She said, "Daddy, why would you want to change what God considers to be perfection?" She told me that **she** loved me the way I was and pleaded with me not to change one hair on my head.

What was wrong with me? I had made my daughter cry. She had more wisdom in one statement than I had in my whole way of thinking. More hair wasn't the answer. The answer was sitting right in front of me, but at that time I was still too blind to see. I asked myself, *"I'm aging and what is so wrong with that?"* On that day I started to learn to accept who I was and who I would become physically. I decided that instead of getting more hair, I would have some taken off. I scheduled an appointment with my hair stylist, but in my case, I regarded her as somewhat of a hair minimalist.

April, 1998
New Jersey
Through The Cuts Of Others, We Learn

Her name was Jan and she had been cutting our hair for about five years. She was excellent. My kids liked her, Georgina liked her and I liked her. We became friendly over the years and talked about anything and everything.

I came in to the salon and Jan started to look at me in a peculiar way. After a few awkward moments I said to her, "So Jan, what's new?" I guess I must have struck a chord, because in a very excited manner she replied, "So, what do you think?"

I didn't know to what she was referring. She obviously wanted me to notice something, but I didn't see anything different so in the fashion of a typical man, who ignores what he doesn't see, I said to her, "I don't know, uhm, just take a little off the bottom." I couldn't say the top because I didn't have anything to spare up there.

She looked at me, dumbfounded, and then said, "My eyes; what do you think of my eyes?" Now I entered a moronic stage, because I didn't know what the hell she was talking about. I thought to myself, *"She's not letting me off the hook, so let me take a stab at this. Maybe she's wearing contact lenses."* My next response to Jan was: "I didn't know you wore glasses but your new lenses look **fabulous**! I can hardly tell you're wearing them."

That was a bust. Jan doesn't wear glasses and wasn't wearing contact lenses. She then said to me, getting a little discouraged, "Don't my eyes look different?" Trying not to insert my foot deeper into my mouth, I told her "I think your eyes are really nice?" (I realize it was a standard male-to-female line, but I was dying there, and I needed to say something at that point).

With relief, she said, "I knew I did the right thing, I had them done earlier in the week." I still looked kind of clued out, so she said, "My eyes! I had my eyes done. It's a new procedure; they inject botulism in between the eyebrows, and magically, it makes the wrinkles go away."

I was completely taken back. I said to her incredulously, "You injected botulism in between your eyebrows? Isn't that stuff poisonous?" She replied, "Normally, yes. But not if they put the right amount in the right place."

I couldn't believe Jan referred to this procedure as magical. The only magical part of this was the stupidity of having something like that done. All of a sudden I completely understood why Gabriella was crying about my hair. That idea must have seemed just as nonsensical to her as Jan's poisonous eyebrows seemed to me.

Then this crazy thought came into my mind. What if she was plucking her eyebrows, and released a lethal dose of botulism onto her husband's toothbrush, then he brushed his teeth and the next thing you know he's removing plaque with angels? What an eye opener that would be!

I now also had a better understanding of why I thought of changing myself for the sake of looking younger and why Jan took steps to do so. We are programmed for it. I don't think it's as bad with men as it is with women, but it's very much there—in every commercial we see on television and every billboard on the street. The message is, "Stay young; young is better."

I made a vow that I was going to do every thing possible to teach Gabriella, Daniel and Rebecca to believe that what they are inside is what counts. I would do everything in my power to show them that if they can bring what's inside of them to the surface, then their outward appearance will be beautiful no matter what age they are.

May, 1998
New Jersey
Sue Me

If I wasn't already comfortable with the way I looked after my talk with Jan, Sue, the swinging nudist, reinforced for me that fooling with nature wasn't a pastime I should be practicing. She had a face-lift and came over after she had the bandages removed to show me how good she looked. I swear I couldn't tell the difference. I told her that she looked great anyway, but it was one of those little white lies that we tell to make someone feel good.

That night Sue ended up in the hospital. She had severe trouble breathing. It seemed that the nose-job part of the beautifying efforts didn't heal well and she needed some medical assistance to clear her nasal passages. I wondered what went through her mind when she decided to have the face-lift. What made her want to risk her health for the sake of so-called beauty?

That was all I needed, I had gotten it all out of my system. I had been looking at myself in the mirror for almost forty years, and if I didn't like what I saw by this time then there was no hope of liking it, no matter what I did. I would just strive to be the best I could be, but at the same time try to be satisfied with who I was. I knew that no face-lift, hair growth, or eyebrow job would help. Maybe some more sleep wouldn't have hurt, but that was not going to happen until Rebecca was about twenty-one years old. Well, maybe more realistically thirty. Would you believe forty?

I wasn't going to let society with all its messages about youth being more desirable, sway this man into thinking that I was not beautiful.

The lines around my eyes show wisdom and character. I choose to look at aging as one of the better parts of living. It brings me closer to understanding all the things that are worthwhile in this world. I would continue the journey and hope that the end result would not disappoint me.

18

ADDICTION

THE CLOCK

THERE'S A NEAT LITTLE CLOCK,
IN THE SCHOOLROOM IT STANDS,
AND IT POINTS TO THE TIME
WITH ITS TWO LITTLE HANDS

AND MAY WE, LIKE THE CLOCK,
KEEP A FACE CLEAN AND BRIGHT,
WITH HANDS EVER READY
TO DO WHAT IS RIGHT.

June, 1998
New Jersey
Steady As We Go

Things were improving between Georgina and me. I think we were getting closer to that middle ground. At least things were heading in the right direction. Georgina's parents were coming into town in a month and she was very excited about that. She hadn't seen them since January and really missed them. They remained in Los Angeles after we left. They had a small income, so it was usually up to us to travel to the West Coast to see them. They were only coming for a weekend, but for Georgina that was better than nothing. It turned out that on that weekend, Georgina's father received quite an education from Daniel.

July, 1998
New Jersey
Do You Smell Smoke?

Georgina's father was in the moving business. He provided written estimates of the cost of a move to potential customers, but once in a while he also drove the moving truck for the company. I guess you could call him a part-time trucker. He is about five feet seven inches tall, a very thin man who was also a heavy smoker.

He had recently cut down his smoking to a couple of cigarettes a day because of the narrowing of an artery in his left leg that was, according to his doctors, a direct result of his tobacco use. He told everyone, including my children, that he had stopped smoking altogether but we all knew he would sneak a smoke or two a day.

When my mother in-law and father in-law came into town that weekend, my father in-law parked his forty-foot truck (much to my neighbor's chagrin) down the street for a couple of days. He had to take a walk to the truck to get something and Daniel wanted to go with him.

He agreed. After they left, Daniel noticed that his grandfather was holding something behind his back. Daniel asked him whether he was still smoking, and hiding a cigarette.

Georgina and I have taught all our children about the evils of smoking and how it can cost you your life. Daniel also understood why his grandfather was having trouble walking, and how that particular ailment was a result of smoking tobacco. Georgina's father told Daniel that he wasn't smoking and there was nothing behind his back. He quickly slipped the cigarette up his sleeve. Luckily, for his sake, it was unlit at the time. Daniel didn't comment anymore about the subject to his grandfather.

After they arrived home, Daniel came to me and told me that he saw his grandfather with a cigarette and thinks he is still smoking. He told me that he thinks his grandfather is in denial. He looked at me with sad eyes and said that he was disappointed that his grandfather had lied to him. He went on to tell me that he understands that his grandfather is addicted to cigarettes and told me, "Pappappa, (that is Daniel's name for his grandfather) should not be embarrassed, I am still proud of him for not smoking as much as he used to."

After I explained to Georgina what had happened, she told her father what Daniel had said. After the initial shock, he had a talk with his grandson and truthfully explained himself. He told me later that he had no idea how perceptive his grandson was, but he wanted to clear up any misunderstanding. He said that he was so worried about Daniel seeing him as a smoker, that he had lost sight of the real danger; his grandson labeling him as a liar.

The interesting part about the whole thing was that Daniel really caused his grandfather to reevaluate his actions. I guess with children, we don't have to be so defensive and we can think more clearly about what we are doing. Maybe the answer to some of the thoughts that still haunted me would come from my children. The whole smoking issue didn't end there. Its ills were reinforced in a very comedic way by a little day trip to New York.

July, 1998
New York City
The Evils Of Smoking

It was such a beautiful weekend in July that we all decided to drive into New York City on the Sunday. We took the New Jersey Turnpike. We arrived at the entrance to the Lincoln Tunnel, entered the toll lane and proceeded up to the ubiquitous tollbooth. (The East Coast's way of sapping every dollar they can out of complacent motorists). There wasn't a lot of traffic, so there were no cars in front of us.

We slowly moved up to the tollbooth and although there was a green light signifying it was open, the window of the booth was unexpectedly closed. An eerie fog-like substance permeated the booth. I felt a chill in the air. The chill may have been the result of the air conditioner blasting directly on me in the car, but I think for artistic reasons, it goes along with the ambiance of the story.

Suddenly, the window of the booth opened and a hand jutted out. It was as if the devil himself was making his play for the very soul of my four-dollar toll. I couldn't see the person attached to that hand: he or she was engulfed in smoke. I did notice, however, a small burning element in the middle of the booth. You could see the burn, and then it would mysteriously disappear. Then reappear, then disappear again.

Before I went too far with my fanciful thoughts, my wild devil story came to an end when we all realized that the person in the booth was what I call, "An All Encompassing Smoker." I concluded that the toll booth operator must have kept the window closed until the last possible moment; that way he or she would not waste even the slightest tobacco residue. It was the ultimate in recycling; addiction at its maximum.

I placed my money in the operator's hand, which was more than the toll. The hand disappeared into the smoke and then re-appeared with my change, closing the window on each exchange. We then drove off and entered the tunnel. What we immediately noticed though, was that the money had a putridly strong smell of smoke. It was disgusting.

We proceeded through the tunnel into the city. We arrived on 34th Street, which was our final destination. I parked the car and we all took a walk. The kids were a little hungry so we stopped at a New York street vendor who was selling hot dogs. I figured this was a good place to get rid of the smoke-infested money.

I handed it to the vendor as payment for the hot dogs. His face quickly gave away his discontentment with the money. Believe it or not he refused to take it. I was in shock. It was like the toll booth operator had created his own foreign currency, which was not accepted in this country. I had to think of a creative way to get rid of those smoky dollars. If a street vendor wouldn't take it, then who would?

Figuring out how I could spend that money consumed my thinking for most of the day. Everyone was suggesting different places to spend that money. I couldn't even put the money in my pocket. I was afraid it would spread its ungodly odor and contaminate the rest of my cash. This was no ordinary smell. It was as strong as a potent spray from a skunk after it was threatened by a dangerous predator. This was really a bad situation. It was truly something from Hell. Maybe my devil story wasn't that far off. Thank heaven I was finally emancipated on the way home. I pawned off all of those smoky bills to other toll booth operators.

After that incident, Georgina's father told me that he promised that he would never smoke while there was hard currency around. I guess when someone is that addicted to anything the thought of stopping entirely doesn't enter their mind, not even in jest.

August, 1998
New Jersey
Summoned to Help

It was a very hot day in August. At seven in the morning, it was already 85 degrees. The kids were still sleeping and Georgina had left for work. The phone rang and it was Sue. She was crying hysterically.

I told her to calm down and tell me what had happened. I was ready to hear her tell me that she had contracted AIDS, or something that was just as horrible (after all Sue did lead a very promiscuous life), but that's not what she told me. She had been to a lawyer and had divorce papers drafted.

She asked me whether I would go down to the court with her to help her file for divorce. I thought that this was a positive step in her life, but the whole situation was ripping her apart. She kept repeating to me, "Thirty years. Thirty years of failure."

She knew she had not been happy for a long time, but the thought of failing at her marriage really hurt her. Maybe that was why she stuck it out so long. I told her that I would come with her. I phoned Angela and asked her whether she would watch the kids for a couple of hours while I ran an errand with another friend.

Sue and I went to the family services department at the courthouse, where the county requires you to file the papers. It was the most depressing place I can remember. Women were sitting waiting with their children. Most of them were there to complain that their husbands were not paying child support.

I saw one woman at the counter pleading with the clerk, "We couldn't eat last night. That son of a bitch is out there spending all his money on whores instead of feeding his kids." The clerk just put her hands up and said, "I'm sorry Miss, there's nothing we can do; you have to talk to the Judge." The woman told the clerk that she had been to court numerous times with no result. The clerk finally dismissed her and said "Next."

The whole thing scared me. I never wanted my children to be in that position. Whatever problems I had with Georgina, I was now even more determined to work them out. I came home after I dropped Sue off and called Georgina. I told her that we have to always try to work on our marriage, for our sakes and our kids' sakes. That night she came home early and said to me, "Mark, I am really trying. I love you with all my heart." I told her that I loved her too and we embraced, like we had stepped back in time to a simpler day. Georgina and I were now working on our marriage with renewed dedication and those were steps in the right direction.

Sue was also going to be all right. We had a chance to talk at the family services department while we were waiting to be called for the divorce filing. She told me that from that day on, she would be seeking a monogamous relationship. She was tired of the life she led and felt that this was her chance at a better one. Sue said that going from a very sheltered environment as a child and teenager to a marriage of unrealistic expectations, sent her down a road of disappointment. She felt that now, after twenty plus years of a bad marriage behind her, she was a lot wiser. I was really happy for her.

September, 1998
New Jersey
Fifty Percent Of All Americans

It looked like divorce was on the rise within my own little sector of friends. Hallie, our former next-door-neighbor, called from Los Angeles. We hadn't heard from her for at least two years. She told me that she and Harry were divorced. I was shocked. I thought that they should have changed babysitters, but I never expected a divorce. Hallie told me that it was a crushing blow to Missy, even though they ended the marriage civilly. I felt so bad for Missy. Aside from the divorce, and the previous maids with which she had to deal, there were a lot of other problems.

Hallie said that Harry was so depressed after the breakup of their marriage that he had become an alcoholic. He struggled with alcoholism for a couple of years and apparently was not very nice to Missy. Hallie started dating again and that was also very hard on Missy because she felt she was losing Hallie, after recently losing Harry. Why is everything in these people's lives so complicated? I didn't know what to say to her. I wished her the best and told her that we would make an effort to see her and Missy on our annual trip to California.

19

HEADS UP

SEE, SEE

*SEE, SEE! WHAT DO I SEE?
A HORSE'S HEAD WHERE HIS
TAIL SHOULD BE.*

October, 1998
New Jersey
Brains Not Brawn

I was a month into soccer season and this was my last year of coaching Daniel's team. He would be ready for the travel team next year and since Rebecca would start playing at the same time, it was only fair that she should also have some of my time on the field. Gabriella was doing well on the travel team, but the coach felt that she needed to learn how to head the ball better and asked me to work with her.

I think she was afraid of getting hurt. I tried heading the ball myself and it does hurt, but as an overzealous father I was intent on making her the best ball header in the world. I went out every day with her after school. Then one day Georgina changed my mind when she came home with an article from a recent medical report, which stated that continuously heading a soccer ball could damage the brain much the same way as a boxer who gets hit in the head too many times.

I had worked too hard with my children in their schooling for it to be all taken away because of a piece of leather wrapped around some air. I stopped practicing with her and told her if she didn't head the ball that much it was okay with me.

I think that prompted Gabriella to think about different sports, because one day she called me from school to ask me whether she could participate on the school basketball team. I thought it would be a good idea for her to spread her wings, so I consented, and let her join the team.

She had a practice the same day. I took her to the practice and saw that there were two coaches. One was the gym teacher of the school and the other was one of the parents I knew. His name was Fred. He volunteered to be the head coach of the team, which was okay with me, since I knew him to be a mild man and thought he was good with children.

That night when Gabriella returned home from practice, she was very upset. She told me that while the team was practicing, one of the boys, (this was a co-ed team) was not paying attention. Fred, in the heat of anger, threw a basketball at the boy and just barely missed Gabriella.

Gabriella was afraid of going back to another practice. Heading the ball in soccer seemed much safer compared to this experience. She wanted to quit the basketball team. I am a firm believer in commitment and don't like when you start something and don't see it through, but in this case I made an exception. Gabriella already had a commitment to the soccer team and it didn't seem to me that this would be such a rewarding experience for her.

Gabriella heard from her friends that in subsequent practices, Fred did throw the ball again. The team was afraid of him. Aside from the fact that Fred turned out to be a "think fast/heads up" kind of guy, I decided to use this as a lesson. I explained to Gabriella what I believed that Fred did wrong as a coach. I told Gabriella that Fred had not used understanding. He didn't bother to understand that the kids were tired from a whole day of school and there were other ways of getting their attention without resorting to violence. As the saying goes "You catch more bees with honey."

I also told her that Fred did not use common sense. He could have seriously hurt that boy, or for that matter, if his aim was off, he could have hurt Gabriella. Lastly, I told her Fred did not use any wisdom. He not only alienated her (she quit the team) but he had created fear in the remaining kids and he did not gain their respect for him as a coach.

Our talk went well. Gabriella understood what I had said. I was getting pretty good at this Mr. Mom thing, but before I patted myself on the back too much, I had an incident on the soccer field with Daniel.

Late September 1998
Excitement Takes Hold

The last week in September we had a game and we were undefeated as a team. The coach against whom we were playing was somewhat of a hard-ass. His team hadn't lost yet either and I really wanted to beat him. The game came down to a penalty shot. One of his players had tripped my center forward in the goal box and now my team had a chance to win the game.

Jimmy, a very good player on my team, was capable of making the goal. Before the shot, as the coach, I had a moment to go to him and guide him on how best to take the penalty shot. I was very excited and letting the moment get the best of me, I said to him, "Kick it in the top of the frigging net." I almost said "fucking." I just barely caught myself. I hoped he heard what I actually said and not what I meant to say.

He made the shot and we won the game. After Jimmy had scored, all the parents, the other players on my team and I were jumping up and down with tremendous excitement. When I got to Jimmy's side he said to me, "I did it coach, I put it in the fucking net." I responded, "That was great, Jimmy." I didn't know whether his mother, who was standing right there heard what he had said, but by the look on her face, she might have.

Later that night, I gave what transpired on the field some thought. I imagined that Jimmy went home and said to his mother after the game, "The coach told me to put it in the fucking net and I did it Mom."

What would Jimmy's mother's reaction be? I guess she could always reply, "Good for you son. Damn you, you little bastard, you're the best fucking son I could ever have." On second thought, I think her reaction would have been more like, "If you ever repeat what that crass, uncouth man that you have for a coach says again, I will wash your mouth out with soap." Poor Jimmy, I wasn't much of a role model.

I learned another lesson. I had to be much more careful not to let myself get so involved in the game. I couldn't allow myself to forget that there are children playing out on that field and not a bunch of foul-mouth adults. Now that I think of it, maybe we adults should treat each other with the same restraint that we try to afford to the children.

20

THE AWAKENING

FROM LITTLE THINGS

LITTLE DROPS OF WATER,
LITTLE GRAINS OF SAND,
MAKE THE MIGHTY OCEAN
AND THE PLEASANT LAND.

October,1998
New Jersey
Switching Gears

I went out for lunch with Angela and told her the soccer story. She enjoyed many of the stories and thoughts that I had about the children. I would also talk to her about my feelings of inadequacy. She was a very trustworthy friend and a good listener. On that day she made a suggestion. She told me that since I had more time on my hands, because all my children were in school, as a therapeutic venture I should write down all my stories and thoughts and it might help me work out a few things that had been troubling me.

Usually I would resent someone trying to play therapist and reject any suggestion offered immediately, but this time I thought, maybe it wouldn't hurt. If I could see my life in black and white, then I might view things from a different perspective. After all, the last forty years would only take a couple of paragraphs. I went home and started making a list. I went all the way back to when I was a teenager, before I left Toronto.

As I started to put the last twenty or so years onto paper, I noticed that whatever I did, I did because I chose to do it. I chose to drop out of school, I chose to move away from Toronto and I chose to become Mr. Mom. I didn't have to do those things; I chose to do those things. The question was why? Why did I choose to follow paths that I was at odds with? Why didn't I do something else with my life? The answers to those questions were staring up at me on those pages and it would only take a few more months for me to clearly see them.

November, 1998
On A Lighter Note?

Soul searching was hard work, but it was time for me to get back to reality. Three children and a wife to take care of was no small matter. Things seemed to be deteriorating for Georgina at work. We spent many hours talking about strategies on how to get around certain destructive situations. She was becoming more and more disappointed with the way her boss was treating her. We were under siege mentality.

At home Gabriella was experiencing a tough year in school. The girls in grade six ostracized her after she wouldn't conform and take on *Cosmopolitan* as her bible. Rebecca and Daniel thank heavens, were easier. They were enjoying their days in school and seemed, for the most part, happy. Friday was approaching and in keeping with the Jewish Sabbath, it was my time to cook a special weekly dinner.

Gabriella calls it a feast. We sit at the dining room table to set the night apart from the other nights of the week when we often just grab a quick dinner in the kitchen. Georgina decided a long time ago not to make it a religious event, but to make Friday nights our family night. Everyone gets a chance to tell how his or her day or week was and express anything else that is on our minds.

It is almost like a show-and-tell, but without the show. I literally mean everyone gets a chance, including Georgina and me. The children looked so forward to this time, not only to tell what interested them, but also to hear the things that Georgina and I do and think about. Sometimes, after dinner, the kids actually put on little plays with costumes, props and all. Friday nights are truly special in our house.

This particular Friday was different from the others. Georgina and Gabriella were each going through a very trying time and Gabriella especially could not hold back her tears that night.

Late November 1998
Crisis Is At Hand

The evening started out like any other Friday. We were sitting at the table and Daniel was telling all of us how his day went. When the turn passed to Gabriella, she sat there for a moment and didn't say anything. I could see her eyes pooling up. She swallowed heavily, trying desperately to hold back the tears. When she opened her mouth, she couldn't utter a word. She completely broke down. Tears started flowing from her dispirited eyes. Georgina began crying too. Then Daniel and Rebecca, not to feel left out, followed suit. Georgina immediately went to comfort Gabriella, but she was so disconsolate, that she left the table and ran up to her room.

With Daniel and Rebecca crying and Georgina now trying to comfort them, I went upstairs to talk to Gabriella. After calming her down a little, I asked her what hurt her so deeply. I knew what the answer was, but she needed to talk and tell me again how the other girls in her sixth grade class were treating her badly. She said to me, "Daddy, I sit alone at lunch every day. I'm lonely in school."

I had to do something about the situation. It was breaking my heart to see my little girl so miserable. We talked half the night. Then Gabriella asked me something that helped me solve her problem. She asked me why the girls couldn't be more like the boys. She told me that the boys didn't judge her and didn't care what she wore each day. Gabriella said that she thought the boys were nicer.

I said to her, "Gabriella, why don't you sit with the boys at lunch?" She was taken aback. She replied "The boys! Daddy I couldn't sit with the boys, no girls sit with the boys."

I told her that if I had lunch with the girls, she could have lunch with the boys. The boys could be her friends. I urged her to find the courage to sit with them. I said, "It's really what the boys want. I know because

I was once a boy." I told Gabriella to sleep on it and we would talk more in the morning.

On Monday, Gabriella told me that she was going to try and sit with the boys at lunch, but she was very nervous. That day when Gabriella came home, her face showed everything. She was excited and said to me, "It worked; I sat with the boys!" She explained that she went over and sat with the boys and they asked her why she was there. She told them that she thought that they had interesting things to say. They decided to let her stay.

At that point I wasn't sure that my idea was so great after all. Gabriella's ability to talk to boys that way scared me a little. It looked liked Gabriella was pretty savvy. I started thinking of her as a teenager. It really scared the hell out of me. I know I'll be the type of father who waits up nervously for his daughter to come home, and if she comes in a minute after her seven o'clock curfew, she's in deep trouble. Isn't seven fair? I began to imagine Gabriella coming home and saying to me, "Dad this is my boyfriend Robert; he just asked me to go steady." That is when I will put all my efforts into developing the full body chastity belt for the well-dressed teenager.

On the next Friday, everything was much better with Gabriella. She told us that one of the boys even protected her when a girl treated her rudely. Gabriella explained that one of the girls said that instead of twelve boys in the class now there were thirteen, insinuating that Gabriella was a boy. One of the boys called this discourteous girl a loser and apparently she cowered away into oblivion. I was very happy that it had worked out so well. I wished that Georgina's problems at work would be that easily solved.

December, 1998
The Journey Continues

I kept writing down a list of events in my life and found that I was staring at the paper. I saw nothing. I felt that the answers to my insecurities were there, but I just couldn't perceive them. Hidden within those words that I had written was a diamond, but it was placed in a glass bowl, filled with water. I knew it was there, but I was not yet discerning enough to view the facets of that stone. I was determined not to give up. If there was something between those lines that would make me feel better about myself, then it was worth pursuing.

December, 1998
The Company Party

It was that time of year when everyone was getting into the holiday spirit. Georgina's department had their annual Christmas party and although she didn't feel like going, she forced herself. The day after the party I decided to meet her for lunch. I hadn't done that in a long time and I thought it was long overdue.

When I arrived at her work, her boss, who was visiting the site, saw me and came over to say hello. He told me what a nice time they had at the party the previous evening and he wanted to know whether Georgina was okay, because he was very concerned about her well being. This was the same man who had said to Georgina, "Putting your heath aside..." He was fishing and I didn't give him an inch. I don't know what he had up his sleeve, but whatever it was, Georgina and I would remain strong together.

I found Georgina, and we had a very nice lunch. That evening I thought about the strength that Georgina and I had when we stood together as a couple, and remembered some of the things that I wrote on my list.

Went to Los Angeles together with my brother Joel
Georgina and I were married together in New Jersey
Georgina and I moved together to Los Angeles
Gabriella, Daniel, Georgina, and I moved together to New Jersey

I noticed that whenever I listed any big event in my life, such as a move across country, I always put the word "together" in the sentence. Georgina and I were married *together* in New Jersey. Even before I married Georgina, I used that word with my brother Joel. Went to Los Angeles *together* with my brother Joel. I realized that having unity was very important to me. In the critical events throughout my life, I had been striving for real unity; with my brother, my father, my wife and children, and my friends.

I guess it was something in my upbringing. My father always told me that together we are strong, alone we would not survive. I knew that I had now seen one piece of the puzzle. The second piece would come at a Christmas party that was thrown by one of Georgina's closest friends.

21

REGRETS, I'VE HAD A FEW

THE WISE OLD OWL

A WISE OLD OWL SAT IN AN OAK.
THE MORE HE HEARD, THE LESS HE SPOKE;
THE LESS HE SPOKE, THE MORE HE HEARD.
WHY AREN'T WE ALL LIKE THAT WISE OLD BIRD?

Late December, 1998
New York City
Christmas Cheer

It was near the end of December and every year, Janice, a close friend of Georgina's, gave a holiday party that we tried to attend. I called Nathan, our babysitter, and asked him whether he was available that Saturday night. Nathan was getting older and it was becoming more difficult to grab some of his time, but luckily he was free that night.

When we arrived at the party, I immediately recognized the cast of characters. They were usually the same from year to year. Janice was very eclectic with her choice of friends. It was a very diverse group.

Over in one corner, you had your snooty New York crowd, the ones that have an opinion on everything and engage in rapid-fire verbal Ping-Pong and say things to each other like: "Well, the exhibition at the Met was the one to see," "Oh, No!! The Museum Of Modern Art put it to shame this year; What are you possibly thinking????" I usually move quickly past that side of the room and never hear which museum is ultimately triumphant.

On the other side of the room were the people who worked for the City of New York, in the family law courts. These were the good-hearted souls who dedicated their lives to helping abused children make their way through our over-loaded court system, and tried to settle them into a better life.

Located right in the middle of the room, were Jan's friends from photography school. They were emotional, artistic human beings who would cry spontaneously if you criticized their work. Maybe that's why they were wearing dark sunglasses indoors on a snowy December evening. It was quite a group, but I was there to make the best of it and I wouldn't let anyone bother me.

About twenty minutes after Georgina and I arrived at the party, a man arrived. Jan brought him over and introduced him to me. "This is

Jim," she said. "I think you guys would enjoy talking to each other." There was really no other game in town so I thought, "*Why not? I have to kill an hour or so anyway.*"

Jim told me that he was 56-years old, divorced for about five years and had attended the party with a woman he had been dating for about three years. Why he was telling a perfect stranger all this information about himself was beyond me, but for some reason I wanted to listen. Jim let me know in the first ten minutes of our conversation how much he loved the woman whom he had brought to the party.

I guess he wanted to establish that piece of information quickly. He told me that he had two sons from his marriage; one was a lawyer and the other a doctor. He told me how very proud he was of them and what a wonderful relationship he had with each of his sons. The conversation was now getting closer to home. I had achieved that kind of relationship with my Dad and I was interested, from a father's point of view, to learn what went on inside his mind to enable him to attain that level of affinity with his sons.

I interjected at that point and told Jim that I thought he was very lucky, because that accomplishment was one of the most important things that you could ask for in life. He then opened up a little more and started telling me about his wife. Early on in their marriage, she was diagnosed as a schizophrenic. Although they had tried different medications over the years, she was in and out of hospitals during the course of their entire life together.

Jim cared for her for 25 years. He told me that even though it was a burden on him, he felt it was important to keep the family together. That's the way he was brought up; family was of the utmost importance.

In the later years Jim's wife became very sick. He finally had to put her in a group home. Jim told me that it was not a hospital, but rather a place where people with similar conditions lived together and received the care they needed. Once Jim's wife became comfortable and happier in her new life, to his surprise, she urged and pleaded with him to get a divorce so he could move on with his life.

Jim told me that at first he didn't know what to do. He had cared for his wife for so long he thought that **was** his life's purpose. He also didn't know how his sons would view that kind of decision. He talked to his sons about the idea of divorce. He told me it was a very emotional time for them. Jim was torn between the prospect of moving on with his life and what he viewed as his responsibility to the woman he married. He thought about the commitment he had made to his wife to be with her "in sickness and in health." His two boys made it very clear that they wanted to see their father happy and they respected him for the courage it took to keep the family together.

After much agonizing, Jim agreed to the divorce. He told me that initially he regretted it. Jim felt that he had failed in his commitment. I could see that he was still having trouble living with his decision of divorce. At that point in the story, I stopped him again. I asked Jim if he was happy now. He replied "Yes, very." I told him that I thought that what he did had made him the man he was today and that man had accomplished the relationships with his sons and the relationship with the woman who was with him at that party.

He should have no regrets. He loved his wife and he had fulfilled the commitment he had made on their wedding day. She released him; now he should release himself. As soon as I told Jim to release himself I got the chills. Was I talking to myself? Wasn't I carrying around baggage that I had to set free? Like a light bulb coming on in my mind a second piece of my puzzle just appeared. My list!

Dropped out of school

Was a homemaker

All the things I did that I had thought disappointed my father were not relevant anymore. He had released me. I needed to release myself, just like Jim. I talked to Georgina that night about my conversation with Jim and what I had learned. I was getting closer to the answer that would set me free and allow me obtain the inner peace that I craved.

December, 1998
Los Angeles
Back to the Beginning

Two days after Jan's party, Georgina, Gabriella, Daniel, Rebecca, and I were all on an airplane headed toward the West Coast for our annual California trip. I was really looking forward to seeing my parents. We were spending the first part of the trip in Los Angeles and then going to Palm Springs for a couple of days at the end.

While we were in Los Angeles, Georgina thought we should get together with Hallie. We hadn't seen them in a very long time and Missy was very anxious to spend some time with Gabriella.

We met Hallie and Missy for dinner at an open-air food court in a mall at Century City. It is the area in Los Angeles where 20th Century Fox has its movie and television studios and the mall used to be the back lot of the studio. Things had changed. Hallie brought a man with her. She introduced him as her fiancée. She was very excited and told us that she was getting married again. She looked good and seemed very content.

Hallie's fiancée seemed to be a very nice guy who cared very much for Hallie and Missy. Missy looked a little happier, although she had gained quite a bit of weight since the last picture we had received. Hallie told us that her ex-husband Harry had finally entered a good rehab program. She said that he had been sober for some time and had become a much more attentive dad.

He took Missy twice a week and apparently she was glad to spend time with her father. I was gratified to see things working themselves out. I thought Missy was a nice girl who deserved a little happiness.

While I was talking to Hallie a funny thing happened. In the middle of the conversation she stopped me cold. Out of nowhere she asked me in a very serious way: "What do you think is the meaning of life?" The way the question was posed took me by surprise. I just sat there for a moment thinking about the question that has puzzled all of mankind through the ages. How was I supposed to answer that? I was searching for the same thing.

Then I looked at Missy, Hallie's new fiancée, Georgina, Gabriella, Daniel, and Rebecca and had a moment of lucidity. I looked at her and said "To love and be loved. To allow your heart to grow and develop as many branches as possible so in some positive way you can touch other hearts." She looked at me and smiled. I don't know what she got out of my answer, but I had the final piece to my puzzle. I didn't need to go back to my list; I had my answer.

22

WHEN ALL IS
SAID AND DONE

JOG ON

JOG ON, JOG ON, THE FOOTPATH WAY,
AND MERRILY JUMP THE STILE;
A MERRY HEART GOES ALL THE DAY,
A SAD ONE TIRES IN A MILE.

January, 1999
Palm Springs
The Pieces Come Together

We arrived in Palm Springs and my mind was full of anticipation. I was looking forward to running with my father. When we ran together we talked a lot. Running was something that I had with him that gave me pure gratification. I wanted to talk to him about my revelation in life, what I had discovered, and how it had put my mind at peace.

My mother was at the door to greet us and I smelled the familiar *Mrs. Dash* chicken permeating from the kitchen. *Mrs. Dash* is a combination of spices that the supermarkets began selling years ago. As soon as my mother discovered it, she began using it in her cooking. *Mrs. Dash* eggs, *Mrs. Dash* potatoes, *Mrs. Dash* asparagus, *Mrs. Dash* EVERYTHING. I would try to sneak other spices into the cupboard, but my mother was blind when it came to other seasonings. I didn't mind so much; there were always restaurants.

The kids loved it in Palm Springs. There was a pond in the back of the house that was filled with ducks. They were very anxious to feed those ducks as soon as possible. The ducks came right up to the house and almost let you hand-feed them. My parents hated the ducks because of what they left as a going away present on the lawn. It was also inevitable that the kids would track some of the duck crap into the house.

I went to sleep early that night, while Georgina and the kids stayed up late talking to my mother. I wanted to get an early start with my father. I was planning on taking a long run.

The morning didn't come soon enough. When I came out of the room where we were sleeping, my father was already in his running clothes and had his warm lemon water, which was his traditional before-run drink. He said to me, " Are you ready?" I was ready; I was more than ready. We started off by stretching outside by the garage. After about fifteen minutes of loosening up, we started to run.

I had a lot to tell him. We started talking about Gabriella, Daniel and Rebecca. He said to me, "You've done a great job with the kids. You've given your mother and me such joy. We are both so proud of you." I thanked him. My father went on to say, "Mark, tell me what's on your mind."

I told him about the list I had made and how, from that list I learned that unity was very important to me. It was one of the reasons that I stayed at home. I wanted to create that oneness with my family. I also explained that I realized that I had been freed from all the misconceptions that were taught to me about being a "man" and how those things put me at odds with what I was doing in my life. I thanked my father for his part in that liberation. Lastly and most importantly, I told him that I now understood that I chose to be "Mr. Mom." It was always in my heart to grow other hearts and now I was free to accept who I was; and I liked that person.

I looked at him, not knowing exactly how he would respond to what I had just said. He responded with a question. He asked me, "What do you want to be when you grow up?" I was confused with that question. I said, "What do you mean?" He restated his question, "When you're my age, how do you see yourself?" To *that* question, I knew the answer and all the strain of running seemed to disappear. I didn't know where I was and I didn't care.

I looked at my father and said, "I want to be like you. I want to be talking to MY children and knowing that they feel about THEIR father, like I feel about YOU." The tears were right there, but somehow we both held them back.

My father smiled with weepy eyes and said, "Let's go this way. You're really going to love this route." I wasn't sure if he was talking about where we were running or where I was heading in life, but at that moment they both seemed gratifyingly sweet.

We returned to the house and I felt that life had really blessed me. I was the luckiest man in the world. That night as we all sat around the dinning room table, I looked at my mother, my father, Georgina, Gabriella, Daniel, and Rebecca and what came to my mind was an old saying: "What goes around comes around."

I had finally realized that I had put my efforts into the only truly important things in life. I was living life with heart and what I was getting back was feeling like a warm breeze on a beautiful summer night, which was penetrating through to my very soul.